HORRIBLE HISTORIES

MEASLY MIDDLE AGES

TERRY DEARY
ILLUSTRATED BY **MARTIN BROWN**

■SCHOLASTIC

With sincere thanks to Helen Greathead

Scholastic Children's Books,
Euston House, 24 Eversholt Street,
London, NW1 1DB, UK

A division of Scholastic Ltd
London ~ New York ~ Toronto ~ Sydney ~ Auckland
Mexico City ~ New Delhi ~ Hong Kong

First published in the UK by Scholastic Ltd, 1996
This edition published 2007

Some of the material in this book has previously been published in Horrible Histories
The Massive Millennium Quiz Book/Horribly Huge Quiz Book

Text copyright © Terry Deary, 1996, 1999
Illustrations © Martin Brown, 1996, 1999
All rights reserved

10 digit ISBN 0 439 94401 5
13 digit ISBN 978 0439 94401 4

Printed in the UK by CPI Bookmarque, Croydon

10

The right of Terry Deary and Martin Brown to be identified as the author and illustrators of this work respectively has
been asserted by them in accordance with the Copyright, Designs and Patents Act, 1988.

This book is sold subject to the condition that it shall not, by way of trade or otherwise be lent, resold, hired out, or otherwise
circulated without the publisher's prior consent in any form of binding or cover other than that in which it is published and without
a similar condition, including this condition, being imposed on a subsequent purchaser.

Contents

Introduction 5

Timeline 7

Nasty Normans 11

Feudal fellows 19

Dreadful disease 30

Nutty knights 42

Awful Angevins 52

Foul food 62

Lousy Lancastrians 73

Woeful women 83

Cheerless children 93

Middle Ages mind-benders 107

Rotten religion 112

Epilogue 127

Grisly Quiz 129

Interesting Index 137

Introduction

History is horrible. Horribly confusing at times. People can't even agree what happened yesterday . . .

> AND THEN I SCORED A BRILLIANT GOAL!

> THE BALL WENT IN OFF YOUR BUM!

When events happened last year, last century or hundreds of years ago we have no chance of knowing the whole truth . . .

> THERE WERE MORE WOMEN IN THE MIDDLE AGES THE POOR MEN DIED IN BATTLE

> NO! THERE WERE MORE MEN DUMBO, THE POOR WOMEN DIED IN CHILDBIRTH

> TO BE HONEST HISTORIANS HAVE ARGUED BOTH WAYS

> HUH! THEY CAN'T *BOTH* BE RIGHT!

You see the problem? Queen Isabeau was described as a tall, short, dark, fair woman, while French peasants were starving, well-fed, smelly people who had regular baths. Historians and teachers have usually said what they thought and that's not the same as giving the facts.

Who can you believe? No one! Your school-books will probably give you one side of the story . . .

> "KNIGHTS WERE BRAVE AND NOBLE WARRIORS! THEY WERE CALLED SIR"
>
> *(PLEASANT HISTORY FOR THE YOUNG)*

This book will give you the other side . . .

> KNIGHTS WERE IGNORANT, VICIOUS BULLIES! IS THAT WHY *TEACHERS* ARE CALLED 'SIR'?
>
> *(HORRIBLE HISTORY)*

Look at the facts and make up your own mind!

Timeline

410 The Romans in Britain go home. The Early Middle Ages start – usually known as the Dark Ages.

793 First Viking attack is on a monastery where the measly murderous maniacs massacre a few monks.

851 Vikings stay for the winter in England for the first time.

871 Alfred the Great becomes King of Wessex. He rules the south and kindly lets the Danish Vikings rule the north of England.

899 Alfred dead and buried. Alfred the Great becomes Alf-in-a-crate.

1017 Vikings triumph when Knut (or Canute) becomes king of all of England.

1066 Nutty Norman Knights aren't satisfied with living in France. The fighting fellers want Britain too. They invade, and hack English King Harold to bits. Their boss, William the Conker, pinches his throne. Historians usually start the Later Middle Ages here.

1086 Measly meanie William orders a record of all his land and people – so he can tax them. That's how the 'Domesday Book' came about.

1099 European armies set off to capture Jerusalem for the Christian Church. These religious expeditions to the Holy Land are known as Crusades. Away win for Crusaders!

1215 Measly King John gets too greedy for money and power. His barons make him sign the Magna Carta and give power back to the people . . . well, the rich people.

1264 Henry III has trouble with the barons. Rebel leader Simon de Montfort captures him and takes over the country for a year. The royal forces kill Simon within a year and send his head to Lady Mortimer as a gift. (And it wasn't even Christmas!)

1291 The Crusaders are driven out of the Holy land. End of Crusading. Who can these men in cans fight next? Each other!

1303 The Baltic Sea freezes over and starts what we now see as the Little Ice Age (lasts till 1700). Shorter growing seasons –

measly food means hunger and misery for millions.

1315 Floods compared to Noah's flood in the Bible. Ruined crops. Hungrier and miserabler millions. Reports from Europe of people eating cats, dogs, pigeons' droppings and even their own children.

1337 English king Edward III says he's king of France. The French don't agree and so they fight – and fight – and fight (on and off) . . . the start of the Hundred Years War.

1349 The Black Death kills off millions in Europe.

1431 French heroine Joan of Arc is captured after stuffing the English armies in battle. She is burned as a witch.

1453 Hundred Years War ends – 116 years after it started.

1459 Now the English start to fight each other! The Wars of the Roses between the Lancaster family (the red rose) and the York family (the white rose) for the throne of England.

1485 Henry Tudor wins the Battle of Bosworth Field and takes the crown from Richard III.

He unites the red and white roses.

1492 Christopher Columbus discovers America. New World, new age, end of measly Middle Ages (though nothing is ever quite that neat!).

Nasty Normans

The bruised Brits had been battered for a thousand years. In 43 AD the Romans ruined them, in the 5th century Saxons savaged them, in the 9th century the Vikings vanquished them. These were the Dark Ages. (No jokes about them being called 'Dark' because there were a lot of 'knights' around in those days.)

But in 1066 the Normans finally nobbled them. Even teachers know that William the Conqueror landed in 1066 and won the Battle of Hastings. The Nasty Normans took over.

These Normans were Vikings who'd settled in Northern France. They wore pointy hats. And who can blame them? They'd probably heard the story of King Geoffrey of Brittany...

King Geoffrey was on a journey to Rome when one of his hawks attacked a chicken in a tavern yard. The inn-keeper's wife was furious. She picked up a big iron pot and threw it at Geoff. It hit the king on the head and killed him. The nasty Normans nipped in and nicked Geoff's land for themselves – wearing helmets to avoid low-flying pots, of course.

The Normans had more writers and monks to record the history of their times. We are no longer 'in the dark' so much. We've left the Dark Ages and entered the Later Middle Ages.

The measly Middle Ages when times were tough and life was hard. Measly food and a measly death by plague ... or war ... or torture ... or simply overwork.

> I GOT THROUGH IT ALL. THE FAMINES, THE FIGHTING, THE BLACK DEATH AND THE GRINDING HARD WORK

> HOW OLD ARE YOU?

> TWENTY FIVE

And you think homework, school dinners and history lessons are bad?

Bloodthirsty Bill

Bill the Conqueror was Norman leader in 1066. He said King Edward of England had promised him the English throne – King Harold said the same thing. It was a fight to the death for two tough fellers. The English must have hoped Harold would win because Big Bill was bloodthirsty ...

- William of Normandy was teased because he was said to be the son of a tanner – a leather-worker. When he attacked Alençon in France in 1048 the people poked fun at him by hanging out skins and shouting, 'Plenty of work for the tanner's son.' This may not have upset *you* – but it made Big Bill furious. He attacked and took 34 prisoners. He paraded them in front of the town walls. As the people of Alençon watched he had their hands and feet cut off and lobbed over the wall. 'That's what'll happen to you if you don't surrender,' he promised. They surrendered.

- William led an army against the Count of Arques. But he marched so fast that he arrived outside Arques town with just six men. The count was waiting with 300 knights. William charged at the Count who turned and galloped for the safety of the town. The 300 knights fled after him. And the Count was William's uncle!
- William wanted Maine in France as well as England. Walter of Mantes claimed both of them, too. Willy captured Wally and his wife and locked them up at Falaise where they died. Some historians say they were poisoned!
- When Will conquered England his reign was harsh. One historian of the time wrote that 'devils had come through the land with fire and sword'. But kind William abolished the death penalty. His last law said, 'I forbid that any man be executed or hanged for any offence, but let his eyes be gouged out.' Of course when an English earl called Waltheof rebelled in 1076 William *forgot* that law. Will gave Walt a chop at Winchester. Measly.

I WISH SOMEONE WOULD REMIND HIM

- Some English rebels didn't know how cruel William

could be. They soon found out in the North of England. When Will and his Normans marched on York every English man and boy they met was slaughtered. The army was broken up into smaller wrecking parties. Anything of any use to a human was destroyed – houses burned to the ground, crops burned, cattle killed and farm tools broken. From York to Durham a whole generation of people were wiped out. The roads were scattered with corpses and some said the survivors turned to cannibalism to stay alive. In 1086 York was still almost deserted.

You'll be pleased to know that when Billy the bully tried to do the same to a town called Mantes his horse trod on one of the burning cinders and stumbled. The fall hurt William's great gut and he died in agony.

Family feuds

The Normans didn't like the English – in fact they didn't even like their own family! William the Conqueror's brother, Odo, looked after England while Bill popped back to Normandy. What thanks did Odo get? William threw him in jail!

But Bill's sons were worse. They fought against each other and they even fought against their dear old dad.

William the Conqueror probably couldn't write – he had clerks to do that for him. But if William could have written a letter to his wife Matilda in 1079...

> Gerberoi Castle
> Normandy
> January 1079
>
> Dearest Matilda
> You won't believe what our Robert has gone and done! Only gone and beaten his dad in battle thats all! The ungrateful little swine (oops! Pardon my French.)
> As you know he was rebelling against my rule so I rode up to Geberoi with a few hundred lads to sort him out. What does he do? He locks the gates. What do I do? Well, I besiege him don't I? A few hungry weeks without his venison pasties and he'll come begging for mercy, won't he. Always been fond of his grub has our Robert.
> But he doesn't! Instead he gets his forces together and comes charging out of the castle! He attacks me! I thought I was supposed to be attacking him!

Of course he's made a big mistake. No one has ever beaten your William in battle as you know. He charges straight for me. Took me by surprise, that did. Knocked me clean off my horse. (Don't worry, my love, he didn't hurt me very much).

The rest of his men began moving in for the kill when that English lad, Toki, rides up with a fresh horse and saves my life. Poor young Toki got killed, but the main thing is I survived.

Now, I don't want to worry you, my darling, but our young Will was fighting on my side and he took a bit of a knock. He's recovering nicely and he's quite a hero. I always thought he was a useless little twerp until now, as you know. But I've decided to give him the throne of England when I go to that great throne in the sky.

As for Robert, he can have Normandy... and the ungrateful little beggar is welcome to it.

Home soon, my dearest one

William
(Conqueror)

> Normandy
> January 1079
>
> Dear William
>
> Just wait till I see our Robert. Fancy knocking you off your horse. He needs teaching some manners. Mind, I always did say you spoilt that boy something rotten. A few whacks with the flat of your sword would have done him no harm at all.
>
> And I suppose you needed Toki's help because you are getting too fat to get back on your horse by yourself. When you get home you are going on a diet my lad.
>
> Do you think you could remember to bring me some of that local woollen cloth? Green if you can get it.
>
> Hurry home. The dogs are missing you, and I'm keeping your throne warm.
>
> Love, Matilda
>
> P.S. Don't forget to wipe your feet before you come into the great hall. I've just had new rushes put down.

William forgave Robert enough to leave him Normandy. But when old William died, young William Rufus got England. This caused a lot of quarrels between the brothers. Each wanted what the other had! A third brother, Henry, got just 5,000 pounds of silver. Who came off best?

Henry, actually.

William Rufus was killed by an arrow when he was out hunting in the New Forest – though some historians think measly Henry might have arranged that 'accident'. Henry took William's English throne, crossed over to Normandy and defeated Robert in battle and took Normandy too.

Henry had the lot. William the Conqueror would have been proud of his murdering, fighting, ruthless son!

The fatal forest

The story about William Rufus being shot in the New Forest is quite well known. His brother, Henry, is suspected of murder because he was in the same forest at the time of William's death.

But, strangest of all is the fate of Richard. Richard who? Richard was the fourth son of William the Conqueror. In 1074 Richard was killed in a riding accident . . . guess where? That's right – in the New Forest.

Richard came to a very painful end. He was charging through the forest on his horse when he collided with a tree. (There were no driving tests for horse riders in those days. If there had been then Richard would have failed.)

Richard was carried back to Winchester, but his injuries were so bad that he died soon after.

William the Conqueror was really upset. (And the tree can't have been too happy either!)

Feudal fellows

The Normans brought the 'feudal system' with them. The king was at the top of the heap and peasants at the bottom. They paid for everything – they worked in his fields, worked in his castle, repaired his roads... all for free. The peasant then worked on a small patch of his own land in his spare time – not a lot of *that*. If the peasant made any money then he paid taxes to his lord. He paid the lord for grinding his corn, pressing his apples or baking his bread in the measly lord's oven.

The feudal system

> I'M A VILLEIN. MY LORD LETS ME LIVE ON HIS LAND. IN RETURN I WORK FOR HIM. I'M A SLAVE – THE LOWEST OF THE LOW

> AND I'M EVEN LOWER THAN YOU

> I'M A FREE PEASANT. I FARM THE LAND OWNED BY MY LORD. IN RETURN I PAY HIM RENT. I'M POOR AND MISERABLE

> I'M POOR, MISERABLE *AND* OVERWORKED

> I'M A KNIGHT. I GET MY LAND FROM THE KING. IN RETURN I FIGHT FOR HIM WHEN HE NEEDS ME. NOTHING BUT FIGHT, FIGHT, FIGHT.

> AND WHO HAS TO LOOK AFTER THE LANDS WHILE HE'S AWAY? POOR ME!

> I'M KING. I GET MY LAND FROM GOD. IN RETURN I SAY PRAYERS, BUILD CHURCHES AND FIGHT FOR HIM. BUT THERE'S ALWAYS SOMEONE AFTER MY THRONE

> AND I'M ALWAYS TRYING TO GIVE HIM SONS TO CARRY ON THE ROYAL FAMILY. WHAT A LIFE

> I'M GOD. I THOUGHT I'D MADE ALL THESE CHAPS EQUAL. MAYBE MY OTHER SERVANT WILL SORT THIS OUT FOR ME...

> I'M DEATH. THEY'RE ALL EQUAL AS FAR AS I'M CONCERNED. BUT A DOSE OF PLAGUE WILL DO THEM THE WORLD OF GOOD

And the plagues of the 14th century certainly changed the world. After the Black Death there weren't so many peasants about! Peasants became rare... and valuable!

> MY DEAR LITTLE WORKING CHAP, WORK FOR ME AND I'LL PAY YOU DOUBLE WAGES

> IT'S MORE PLEASANT FOR PEASANTS AT PRESENT

> THAT'S A BIT BETTER

> BUT REMEMBER, I'LL BE BACK

You'd think the peasants would be better off dead – they weren't! After a peasant died the measly lord took his best possessions . . . after all they had only been 'loaned' to the peasant during his lifetime. No wonder . . .

The peasants are revolting
In the measly Middle Ages peasants had a short life, but a miserable one. If overwork didn't kill you then you could die from ordinary things like a rotten tooth. Storing food over the winter could give you a type of food poisoning. Then there were extra nice diseases to look forward to, like St Anthony's Fire – an arm or a leg would get a burning pain . . . then drop off.

When you died you'd hope to go to heaven, but stories went around that a peasant's soul didn't get to heaven – demons refused to carry it because of the horrible smell. They were *really* revolting!

While the peasants froze in the fields, died in ditches or starved in slums, the rich people had 'fun'. In the 14th century Count Robert of Artois had a very pleasant garden. It had . . .
- statues that squirted water at you as you walked past
- a trapdoor that dropped you on to a feather bed
- a hosepipe that squirted water up ladies' dresses
- a statue that squawked at you like a parrot
- a room that greeted you with a thunder storm as you opened the door

HAVE A NICE RELAXING WALK IN THE GARDEN HE SAID... HA, HA.

No wonder the peasants hated the nobles in their castles. The peasants didn't go to school but they knew one simple sum: 'There are more of US than there are of THEM!' In France in 1358 they decided to take over.

The French rebellion was known as the Jacquerie because...

1 Any peasant was known as a 'Jacques' (a 'John' in English) – a very common name – so it was a revolt of the 'Johns'! Or...

2 They wore padded, boiled-leather jackets as a sort of cheap armour and these jackets were called 'Jacques' – so it was a revolt of the padded-boiled-leather-jackets.

Take your pick. Either explanation could be right – or both could be wrong!

Of course the peasants weren't used to organizing themselves – the nobles were. At first the Jacques murdered a few surprised nobles...

---

22 June 1358 — *The PARIS POST* — **STILL ONLY 25 CENTIMES**

PEASANTS HAVE KNIGHTS IN DAZE!

The brave battling peasant army has a new leader who is leading the jolly Jacquerie to victory. His name is Will Cale and he's just what the proud peasants need – a strong leader and an experienced soldier.

The revolt began four weeks ago when the peasants grew furious that the French king had been captured by the English and the noble knights had done nothing – except run away. Armed with axes, scythes and pitchforks a 10,000-strong army captured over a hundred castles.

Knights fled with their families – or stayed and died. There are reports of Jacques jokes like roasting a knight on a spit – then forcing his wife to eat the roasted flesh!

Amazingly, two enemies, an English knight and a French knight, joined forces to help Meaux when it suffered a Jacques attack. Captal de Buch and Gaston Phoebus said, 'When noble ladies are in danger a knight's gotta do what a knight's gotta do.'

The knights with an armed force of just 120 cut the Jacques to pieces with their weapons. 'Using swords against scythes is cheating,' Will Cale grumbled.

Now there are rumours that Charles of Navarre is leading a fightback in the east. Cool Cale says, 'Charles of Navarre? Charlie's for the chop – you'll see.'

The Paris Post supports their battling efforts.

Our Brave Boys

But Charles of Navarre used one weapon that Will Cale didn't have . . . brains!

22 July 1358 — *The PARIS POST* — **STILL ONLY 25 CENTIMES**

CRUEL CALE CONQUERED

The knights are back in power – where they belong! The Paris Post proudly announces that Wicked Will Cale is dead. The Jacquerie is over! Peace has returned to our troubled towns.

Charles of Navarre's likeable lads faced Will Cale's revolting rats near Paris. Charles suggested that they should talk and Cale, the clot, arrived without a guard. Naturally, Navarre nabbed him and locked him in chains! 'That's cheating!' Cale cried but no one was listening. The leaderless louts of the Jacquerie were massacred – or ran like rabbits.

Cheerful Charles gave Cale the crown he craved – a crown of red hot iron! Then he cut off his hateful head. Now he plans to lead an army of destruction through the region. 'Peasant houses, fields and families will be destroyed!' the noble Navarre promised.

The Paris Post supports the overthrow of the sewer-scented masses and the return of our true leaders.

Champion Charlie

The English peasants were a little way behind the French when it came to rebelling. The English peasants' revolt happened 23 years later in 1381. It wasn't only the French knights who could do a bit of cheating. English King Richard II was pretty good at it too!

The peasants in southern England were so fed up with paying a Poll Tax that they marched on London to see the king. They murdered a few unpopular lords on the way and stuck their heads on long poles . . .

> HOW DO I FASTEN THE HEAD ONTO THE POLE?
> TRY SOME POLE TACKS!
> THAT'S NOT FUNNY

But the lords were probably glad to have their noses well away from the smelly marching feet!

The head of the revolting peasants was called Wat Tyler . . . which could have been a problem . . .

> WHAT'S YOUR NAME?
> THAT'S RIGHT IT IS!
> WHAT IS IT?
> YES!
> ASK A CIVIL QUESTION...

Anyway, Wat's 20,000 rebels reached London and presented their demands...

- No more poll tax
- No more slavery for peasants
- Freedom to use the forests
- Freedom to hunt wild animals

FREEDOM FROM HEAVY SIGNS?

The lords in London promised to give in to his demands. Wat didn't believe them (what a wise Wat!). His army raised their trusty, rusty swords and marched into London, murdered a bishop, a lord or two and as many foreigners as they could get their scythes on. The 14-year-old king (Richard II) perched on a war horse promised Wat his support! Wat believed the king. (Showing he was really an unwise Wat.) The head peasant boasted...

In four days' time all the laws of England shall be coming from my mouth!

But Wat Tyler hadn't read his Horrible History books. He didn't learn from what had happened to Will Cale 23 years before. He agreed to meet the king and his guards at Smithfield.

Some historians say that Wat Tyler began by picking a fight with the king's squire and drew his knife. The Lord Mayor of London (William Walworth) drew his sword and killed Tyler.

The leaderless peasants gave in – just as the French peasants had after Cale's death.

Which just goes to show . . . history repeats itself . . . itself . . . itself . . . itself . . . itself . . . itself . . .

Wat's head was stuck on a lance. The head peasant had become a head-less peasant.

The Saxon streaker

William and his Normans are famous for the Domesday Book – a record of everything everyone owned in England. Once the Normans knew what people were worth then they could tax them. A lot of people forget that the poor people of England knew all about paying tax – long before the Normans arrived.

The most famous tax dodge was the deal made by a famous Saxon streaker called Lady Godiva. Roger of Wendover wrote the first report of her daring deed. Here it is in modern English. What is missing from Roger's version of this famous story?

The good Countess Godiva longed to free the town of Coventry from the misery of heavy taxes. She often begged her measly husband, Earl Leofric of Chester, to free the town of those taxes. The Earl laughed at her. 'Your request is foolish,' he said. 'Don't you see how we need that money? To cut those taxes would be to hurt me. Don't ever mention the subject again.'

WE HAVE A VERY EXPENSIVE LIFESTYLE

But Countess Godiva had the stubbornness of a woman (a very sexist remark that Wendover would not get away with today). She would not stop pestering her husband about the matter until finally he snapped at her, 'Get on your horse, ride naked through the market place in front of all the people. If you do that I shall grant your request.'

Countess Godiva replied, 'If I am willing to do this do I have your permission?'

'You do,' he agreed.

At this the Countess loosened her hair and let it fall until it covered her body like a veil. She mounted her horse and, escorted by two knights, she rode through the market place without being seen except for her fair legs.

When she had completed the journey she happily returned to her astonished husband and was granted her request. Earl Leofric freed the town of Coventry from all taxes.

When the story was repeated a hundred years later a historian added a new character to the story. A fiendish feller called Peeping Tom. While all the other citizens of Coventry went indoors and gave the Countess some privacy, terrible Tom spied on her.

Which just goes to show – don't believe every story you read ... especially history stories!

Did you know ... ?
A knight owned his peasants – they were considered part of his wealth. If you attacked a knight then he'd probably shut himself safely away in his castle. The next best thing to do was to attack his peasants in the villages around. In 12th-century France, Thomas de Marle (nickname 'The Raging Wolf') attacked his father's peasants, cut off their feet or put out their eyes. What a measly way to go!

Dreadful disease

In 1347 Death strolled through Europe with his scythe, mowing some down and missing others. Swish! Swish! In 1349 he sailed across the Channel to the British Isles. The terrified people never knew who was going to be next. As an Italian diary recorded . . .

> There appeared certain swellings in the groin and under the armpit, the victims spat blood, and in three days they were dead

These swellings began to ooze with blood and pus. Purple-black blotches appeared on the skin and you smelled absolutely revolting!

Swell - Spit - Smell - Swish! You were gone.

Death's 'scythe' was the bubonic plague and the piles of bodies grew like chopped straw into a haystack. They were loaded on to carts, dropped into pits – or, in Avignon in France, thrown in the river.

HELLO DEAR, CATCH ANYTHING?

Children were Death's particular favourites when it came to the swish. We now know the real reason for this: if you are an adult then you have had quite a few diseases in your lifetime and build up a 'resistance'; children have had fewer diseases and far less resistance. They die easily.

Of course, preachers said the children probably got what they deserved! One explained . . .

> *It may be that children suffer heaven's revenge because they miss going to church or because they despise their fathers and mothers. God kills children with the plague — as you can see every day — because, according to the old law, children who are rebels (or disobedient to their parents) are punished by death.*

You can see that not much has changed.

DO WHAT I SAY... OR DIE!

Crazy cures

The trouble was that doctors didn't know what caused the plague and they didn't know how to cure it. People mistakenly believed you could catch it by . . .
- looking at a victim
- breathing bad air
- drinking from poisoned wells.

In France they said the English did the poisoning, in Spain they blamed the Arabs. In Germany, suspected poisoners were nailed into barrels and thrown into the river. And everyone blamed lepers!

And the cures were almost as dreadful as the disease. Doctors already had some wacky cures for illnesses. They said . . .
- wear a magpie's beak around the neck to cure toothache
- cut a hole in the skull to let out the devil and cure madness.

WELL AT LEAST HE ISN'T MAD ANY MORE

With something as deadly as the bubonic plague they had no chance! They suggested . . .
- throw sweet-smelling herbs on a fire to clean the air
- sit in a sewer so the bad air of the plague is driven off by the worse air of the drains

PERHAPS THE PLAGUE'S NOT SO BAD AFTER ALL

- drink a medicine of ten-year-old treacle
- swallow powders of crushed emeralds (for the rich)

- eat arsenic powder (highly poisonous!)
- try letting blood out of the patient (when the patient's horoscope was right!)
- kill all the cats and dogs in the town
- shave a live chicken's bottom and strap it to the plague sore

> IT'S BAD ENOUGH THAT I'M DYING WITHOUT LOOKING STUPID TOO

- march from town to town flogging yourself with a whip.

> I DON'T KNOW ABOUT CURING THE PLAGUE BUT IT'S GREAT EXERCISE

The doctors checked the urine of their patients. If there was blood in it then there was no hope.

Some people who caught the plague had a natural resistance to it so they recovered. Others took the only 'cure' that worked – run away from the plague-infested towns into the countryside. The rich people, with country houses, could do this. The poor stayed at home and died.

The real cause of the plague wasn't discovered till just a hundred years ago. And people still don't understand – they think rats carried the plague. Fleas carried the plague germs. They lived on rats and their germs killed the rats.

A dead rat is not very tasty (as children who stay to school dinners will tell you) so the fleas looked for a new 'home'. If there were no rats about then the fleas would hop on to a human and spread the germs to that human. When their new human friend died they'd hop on to another human – maybe the person who'd nursed the first victim. And so it went on.

> I THINK I'VE GOT FLEAS DAD
> SCRATCH SCRATCH
>
> ALL THIS PLAGUE AROUND AND YOU'RE WORRIED ABOUT A FEW FLEAS

Suffering Scots
The plague had its funny side – if you have that sort of sick sense of humour! The Scots hated the English and were delighted to see the plague destroying so many of their old enemy.

They decided 1349 would be a good time to invade – the English would be too weak to defend themselves. As their forces gathered the plague struck. Many Scots soldiers died – many more ran home to their towns and villages . . . taking the plague with them! In the wars between England and Scotland, Death didn't take sides.

Plague dogs
In Messina, on the Italian island of Sicily, people believed that plague death appeared as a large black dog. It carried a sword in its paws and smashed the ornaments and altars in their churches. Many swore they had seen it!

> I ALWAYS KNEW THOSE DOGS WERE UP TO NO GOOD

In Scandinavia the people saw Death as a Pest Maiden. She flew out of the mouths of the dead and drifted along in the form of a flame to infect the next house. (Never give the kiss of life to a plague victim or you'd get singed lips!)

In Lithuania a similar maiden waved a red scarf through the window to let in Death. A brave man saw the waving scarf and sliced off the maiden's hand. He died but the village was saved. The scarf was kept in the local church for many years. (Of course, it could have belonged to some 'armless girl, couldn't it?)

Fantastic flagellants
Some people believed the best way to get rid of your wickedness was to beat the devil out of you. In Europe groups of 200 to 300 people called flagellants went around whipping themselves (and each other) for 33.3 days – the number of years Christ lived on Earth. Apart from the steel-tipped whips, they had to put up with . . .

> No shaving
> No washing
> No change of clothes
> No comfortable bed
> No talking to women

At first the flagellants blamed the priests for the evil of the plague. But the priests fought back with threats to ban the flagellants. So the measly flagellants decided to blame an easier target – the Jewish people in towns. They rushed to the Jewish part of each town and murdered everyone they could find.

In some places, like Worms (in Germany) in 1349, the Jewish people cheated the flagellants of their sport – they set fire to themselves in their houses in a mass suicide. Six thousand died in Mainz that year and not one of the 3,000 Jewish people in Erfurt survived.

Mystic medicine

Of course the Black Death was not the only illness that doctors had to deal with in the Middle Ages.

Since ancient times doctors believed that one of the best ways to get rid of sickness was to let the bad blood out of your body. People of the Middle Ages would pop down to the local barber shop and have a vein opened. (If you wanted to save time you could have your hair cut while you waited!)

How could you spot the local barber shop? There was usually a bowl of fresh blood in the window! (In London this was considered bleeding bad taste and banned in 1307. All blood had to be thrown straight into the Thames.)

Apart from bleeding there were other 'interesting' cures in the Middle Ages. But can you match the right cure to the right illness? Try this test – it doesn't matter if you get them all wrong, actually. None of them works anyway!

ILLNESS

1. RINGWORM
2. GOUT
3. PLAGUE
4. SKIN DISEASE
5. LOSS OF MEMORY
6. SLEEPLESSNESS (INSOMNIA)
7. BRUISES
8. FAINTING
9. BLOCKED UP NOSE
10. BLEEDING INSIDE THE BODY

CURE

a. EAT POWDERED EMERALDS
b. EAT GINGER
c. STUFF MUSTARD AND ONION MIXTURE UP THE NOSE
d. A PLASTER OF BACON FAT AND FLOUR
e. EAT TREACLE
f. WASH THE HAIR IN A BOY'S PEE
g. WEAR A DRIED TOAD IN A BAG ROUND THE NECK
h. COVER SORE SPOT WITH SKIN OF A WOLF
i. APPLY A PLASTER OF GOATS DROPPINGS MIXED WITH ROSEMARY HERB AND HONEY
j. BREATHE IN THE SMOKE OF BURNT FEATHERS

Answers:

1f) Washing in a boy's pee might kill you so it would certainly give your ringworm a nasty shock. (Don't try this at home.)

2i) Warning! Don't try to eat the honey after you've finished with it.

3a) Plague doctors sold powdered pearls or powdered emeralds to very rich parents. This was very healthy for the doctor's wallet.

4h) In the mid-14th century a vicar was caught importing four dead (and smelly) wolves' bodies in a barrel. The idea was that the disease would 'feed' on the wolf skin instead of the human sufferer. Surgeons were furious that a vicar was pinching their job!

5b) Eating ginger for loss of memory is quite harmless. I tried it once. It may even have worked – but I can't remember.

6e) Treacle was the great cure of the 15th century. It cured practically everything – including loss of speech, spotty skin and snake bites. (It was a real star among medicines, hence the song, 'Treacle, treacle little star, how I wonder what you are.')

7d) Bacon fat should be mixed with wild boar's grease if you can get it. The trouble is you'd probably get more bruises fighting the boar. Then you'd have to go out and catch another wild boar . . . and so on! Note: An angry teacher should not be killed for his or her grease. They are wild BORES, not boars.

8j) Make sure the feathers are not still attached to the chicken when you set fire to them. The RSPCA takes a very dim view of this.

> **9c)** 'Snot a very nice cure, this one.
> **10g)** If you are embarrassed by a dead toad hanging round your neck, tell your friends it's the latest fashion. Alternatively you may prefer to bleed to death.

Top tip for teachers

The best way to avoid a hangover is to drink with your hat off. Doctors of the Middle Ages said this allows the harmful fumes to pass out of your head. A hat holds them in and gives you a headache. But if the drink affects your kidneys then here's a beetle brew discovered by John of Gaddesden . . .

> *I cut off the heads and wings of crickets and put them with beetles and oil in a pot. I covered it and left it a day and a night in a bread oven. I drew out the pot and heated it at a moderate fire. I ground it all together and rubbed the sick parts. In three days the pain disappeared.*

(**Health warning**: Make sure you use crickets, or little grasshoppers, and not cricketers in this cure. Try cutting a cricketer's head off and you may get a bat in your measly mouth.)

Arab medicine

Arab doctors were far in advance of European doctors. Their cures showed more understanding of disease and their treatments were more gentle – and usually more successful. They could scarcely believe the way doctors behaved in Europe.

Usama ibn Muniqidh told the story of an Arab doctor. He was treating a knight who had an abscess on his leg; he put a dressing on it. For a woman with a lung disease he prescribed the right sort of fresh food.

Along came a European doctor. 'You have no idea how to cure these people,' he said. First he took an axe and cut the knight's leg off. The knight died.

Then he cut a hole in the woman's skull, removed her brain and rubbed it with salt. The woman died.

'I hope you have learned something about medicine today,' the European doctor said.

'I certainly have,' the Arab doctor replied.

A WORD OF ADVICE MY FRIEND, NEVER GET SICK IN ENGLAND

The first flying doctor

Australians are proud of their 'Flying Doctors' – a medical service in aeroplanes. But the Middle Ages saw Doctor Damien of Stirling in Scotland become the first doctor to take to the air.

Doctor Damien was a hopeless doctor and killed as many as he cured. Measly-brained King James IV gave him lots of money to turn ordinary metals into gold – but he failed. Then in 1504 he tried flying. A writer of the time said . . .

> *Damien took it in hand to fly with wings, so he made a pair of wings from feathers. These being fastened around him he flew from the walls of Stirling Castle, but soon fell to the ground and broke three bones. He blamed the failure on the fact that there were chicken feathers in the wings. He said, 'Chickens belong on a dung heap and not in the air.'*

Luckily King James was a pretty good doctor himself and could patch up Damien. The first flying doctor was no chicken – which is more than can be said for his wings!

Nutty knights

The Normans brought the art of castle-building to Britain. Mounds of earth with a wooden wall protected them from the beaten Brits. As they settled in, the castles became larger and were built of stone because now they were protecting themselves from each other!

Of course, castles weren't built by just any old peasant. They were built by knights. Wealthy and powerful soldiers who wore armour and fought on horse-back. These knights were big bullies who battered British peasants into doing as they were told or fought for the king and battered foreign peasants.

Then knights and kings began to do something disastrous . . . they learned how to read! Now they read stories about an ancient king called Arthur of Britain. And Arthur had a strange idea: knights should be gentlemen. Knights treated ladies with respect but, weirdest of all, they treated their enemies with respect! King Edward III (ruled 1327 till 1377) even created a Round Table just like King Arthur was supposed to have.

A knightly fight now had rules. You didn't sneak up on another knight and stab him in the back, even though that saves a lot of trouble and effort. You had to challenge your opponent to a fight and agree the time and place. This may seem a bit strange to you or me – it's like saying, 'Excuse me, my dear fellow, but would you meet me next Thursday, at noon at the meadow by the river, when I will do my best to beat your brains out?'

> I'M AWFULLY SORRY, I'VE GOT MY BRAINS ALL OVER YOUR NICE CLEAN ARMOUR

But, as the boy who put a drawing pin on the head-teacher's chair said, 'Rules are there to be broken.'

Forget the fairy-tales about knights in shining armour battling boldly to win glory ... or death. In truly horrible historical fashion, the most measly knights of the Middle Ages broke the rules. They cheated.

This true 12th-century story is from Ludlow Castle on the border between England and Wales. We learn not all knights were gentlemen – not all maidens were meek and weak. And, in horrible history, not all stories have a happy ending ...

Midnight terror (or, Terror amid knights)

'Women?' the young knight, Geoffrey, laughed and the sound echoed round the cold stone walls of the dungeon cell. 'They love me. And who can blame them. I'm handsome, strong and brave. Any woman would be proud to be my love!'

The rat twitched his whiskers and scuttled back to its

nest under the straw. 'You don't appear to believe me, Master Rat,' the young man said. 'I'll bet you a piece of stale bread that I'll be out of here within a week!'

Geoffrey turned his head sharply as he heard the rattle of keys in the lock of the cell. He brushed the straw off his jerkin, sat up straight and fixed a smile upon his face. The door swung open and the girl hurried in with a dish of gruel and a mug of ale. Her nose curled back at the smell in the filthy air and she placed the food carefully on the floor. It was the only time she would come within reach of the chained man. Suddenly his chain clattered, his hand shot out and grabbed her wrist.

'Ah!' she cried.

'Hush!' he said quickly. 'Stay just a few moments, Marian,' he went on softly.

'My father will be suspicious,' she said anxiously.

Geoffrey spoke quickly and didn't release his grip on the girl's wrist. 'Yesterday, after you'd gone, his lordship came to see me. He has given me just three days to talk. He wants me to tell him our plans for capturing Ludlow Castle. I would not betray my friends, of course.'

'And after three days?' she asked.

'After three days he will torture me. First he will use hot irons on my face . . .'

'No!' she gasped.

'I can bear the pain,' the young man shrugged, 'but it may spoil my looks. No maiden would marry me with those scars. Or he may gouge out my eyes . . .'

'No!' she gasped. 'His lordship's not a cruel man.'

The prisoner shrugged one shoulder. 'We'll see . . . at least *you'll* see. I won't have any eyes left to see!'

'How can you joke about such a thing?' she asked.

'True. I'd be sad to lose my eyes. I'd never be able to see a beautiful face again. A beautiful face like yours.'

The girl blushed and tore her wrist away from his grip. She hurried from the cell and closed the door. The young man smiled.

The next day she came in and knelt beside him silently. She took a small key from her belt and unfastened the chains that bound his wrists. She slipped a larger key from the ring and pressed it into his hand. 'The key to the outer door,' she muttered.

He touched her hand softly. 'Thank you, Marian. You have saved me and I owe you my life. The only way I can repay my debt is by marrying you.'

The girl looked up, startled. 'You'll take me with you?'

'Ah!' he whispered. 'Not just yet. I need time to get away. I want you to stay here, to cover for my escape as long as you can. I'll return for you a week today. Listen, here's what we'll do . . .'

That night, as the monastery bell tolled midnight, he slipped away from the moon-shadows of the castle and stole a horse from the village below. Within an hour he was ten miles from Ludlow. Within a week he was back, as he had promised.

A ladder hung from the window as he knew it would. It was made of strong leather rope and led up to a window in the west tower. A window that wasn't overlooked by the patrolling guards.

Geoffrey climbed it swiftly and felt Marian's strong hands grasp his wrists and pull him over the stone sill. A candle lit the room and glinted on the knight's excited eyes. Marian gave him a nervous smile and moved towards the window. 'Where are you going?' he asked.

'Down the ladder. Away with you,' she said.

He shook his head. 'We have one or two visitors who want to climb that ladder first,' Geoffrey grinned.

'Visitors?'

'Friends of mine. Friends who want a little revenge on your lord.'

A man's face appeared at the window ledge. Geoffrey pulled him into the room. That man in turn helped a second then a third. In five minutes the room was crowded with hard-faced, leather-jacketed men with soft boots and cruel knives.

'What are you doing?' the bewildered girl asked.

Geoffrey ignored her. Instead he turned his back on her and spoke to the men. 'Kill the guards, throw their bodies over the walls then lower the drawbridge . . .'

'My father's on duty tonight!' Marian cried.

'Kill *all* the guards,' Geoffrey said slowly. 'Our troops will ride in and finish the job.'

Marian opened her mouth but before she could scream a warning the knight had clamped a rough, gloved hand over it. He held it suffocatingly tight until the last man had left the room and closed the door. 'Women are fools,' he sneered at her.

But while he held her mouth closed he couldn't control her arms. She had carefully slipped the dagger from his belt and turned it till the point was under his ribs. With all of her strength she pushed upwards.

His lips went tense and his eyes showed more surprise than pain. There was a soft gurgle in his throat as he fell back against the wall. He remained there for half a minute, clawing helplessly at the thing in his side before he slid slowly to the floor.

Marian hurried to the door and looked out on to the battlements. There were cries of terror as men struggled in the darkness and tumbled from their posts. The drawbridge dropped with a crash and there was the sound of horses clattering into the courtyard.

One man's voice seemed to rise above the other cries. 'We've been betrayed!' the voice wailed. 'Betrayed.'

Marian turned back to the room, walked past the lifeless knight and climbed on to the window ledge. 'Oh, we've all been betrayed,' she said dully. The girl simply leaned forward and let herself drop.

In the dark chaos of the night no one heard one more small cry, one more soft crunching of bone on rock.

Did you know . . . ?
Marian wasn't the only castle-dweller to be betrayed. A robber held in Haverfordwest in Wales became friends with some young squires who were training to be knights. He fixed arrowheads for them and gave them to the boys for their bows. The boys begged that the robber be allowed out for some fresh air – in their care. He took them hostage and used them to bargain for his freedom.

And Marian wasn't the only young woman to die in a fall from a castle. Just over the Welsh border in Abergavenny a young girl fell while trying to catch her pet squirrel that had escaped.

Jolly jesters
Castle life wasn't all dungeons, doom and draughts. There were feasts and entertainments. The chief entertainer was the jester.

A 13th-century writer described the skills a jester needed if he was going to get a job in a royal castle . . .

> **WANTED**
>
> Court jester. Must be able to tell stories, imitate bird songs, catch little apples on knives, do card tricks, play sixteen instruments and jump through four hoops...
> (but not all at the same time)

A jester's little joke

Jesters also had to be quick witted. At the Battle of Sluys (1340) the measly English archers fired so many arrows that the French were driven from the decks of the ships and their fleet destroyed. No one dared tell King Philip VI of France. His jester stepped forward . . .

> OH THOSE COWARDLY ENGLISH
>
> WHY ARE THEY COWARDLY?
>
> THEY DON'T DARE JUMP INTO THE SEA LIKE OUR BRAVE FRENCH SOLDIERS

Reports said that the fish drank so much French blood that if they could talk they would have spoken French!

A terrible tale

Jesters weren't the only entertainers in castles at the time. There were minstrels too. They had heroic tales of knights and dragons and ladies. Of course, they didn't have comics in the Middle Ages but they had cheerful little stories that would have made very good comic strips. Stories like 'Renault and the Dame of Fayel' . . .

> THE BRAVE KNIGHT RENAULT FELL IN LOVE WITH THE DAME OF FAYEL BUT...
>
> I'M MARRIED TO LORD FAYEL, SUNSHINE. SORRY, AND ALL THAT

> WHEN LORD FAYEL FOUND OUT HE CAME UP WITH A PLAN TO GET RID OF RENAULT...
>
> HEY RENAULT! WHY NOT GO AND FIGHT IN THE THIRD CRUSADE?
>
> WHAT A JOLLY GOOD IDEA

> SO, OFF WENT RENAULT TO THE HOLY LAND WHERE...
>
> OUCH! CURSES! I'VE BEEN HIT BY AN ARROW
>
> AND THAT LOT USE POISONED ARROWS

> RENAULT GAVE ORDERS BEFORE HE DIED...
>
> TAKE THIS LETTER ALONG WITH MY HEART TO THE DAME OF FAYEL

AFTER I'VE DIED YOU SILLY CHAP!
SORRY, BOSS
BUT THE EVIL HUSBAND INTERCEPTED THE HEART. HE HAD IT COOKED AND SERVED UP TO HIS WIFE!
HAVE A HEART, LOVE
THANKS, PET
BUT HE GOT A SHOCK WHEN SHE DECLARED...
THIS IS THE MOST DELICIOUS MEAL I'VE EVER EATEN! NOTHING COULD TASTE AS GOOD. I WILL NEVER EAT AGAIN!
MY PLAN HAS FAYELED!
AND THE DAME OF FAYEL DIED HAPPY EVER AFTER
THE END!

Awful Angevins

King Stephen followed Henry I as the last Norman king. Henry Duke of Anjou wanted the English throne and, since he was a bit rough, no one argued with him – not even Stephen's sons.

When old Steve died, in 1154, Henry of Anjou became Henry II – the first Anjou (or Angevin) king. Henry had lots of bright ideas for improving England and one of the first things he sorted out was the law. Now . . .

- Accused people could be tried by the people of their own class – juries. (A bit like your classmates deciding if you are guilty of the crime of slopping your school-dinner custard down Alice Anderson's neck.)
- The king's judges then decided what the punishment should be for the guilty. (A bit like the teacher then deciding you have to mop the custard off her neck and pay to have her dress cleaned. Get it?)
- Townspeople took it in turns to act as 'Constable' to question and arrest suspects. (A bit like a classmate having the job of patrolling the school dining-hall to make sure you keep your custard to yourself in future.)

Cruel crimes
'Crime doesn't pay.' That was the message the law wanted to give to people thinking of a spot of murder, treason or thieving. William the Conqueror may have banned executions but they soon returned after his death.

But even executions were all too soon forgotten, so the officers of the law needed a way of reminding the public to behave itself, like . . .

> *Upon London Bridge I saw three or four men's heads stand upon poles. Upon Ludgate Arch the top quarter of a man is set upon a pole. Upon the other side hangeth the bottom quarter with the leg. It is a strange sight to see the hair of the heads fall off or shrivel away while the gristle of the nose is eaten away and the fingers of the hands wrinkle and wither to the bare bones. It is a sight for all young people and a warning to them that they should behave themselves.*

A schoolteacher came up with this jolly piece of writing! He wrote it as an exercise for his pupils to copy out in Latin – and as more than a little hint to his pupils: 'This is what will happen to you if you don't do as you are told!'

Criminal capers

Henry II's laws were really needed by the poor people of England. While kings and barons fought each other, the bullies in the country took the law into their own hands. The Middle Ages were wild and dangerous times. But it wasn't just the poor peasants who turned to crime . . .

1 Robin Hood may have lived in the royal forests of

Sherwood in Nottinghamshire . . . or he may be an invented character and about as real as Donald Duck. But outlaw Sir Gosseline Denville did exist. After wasting his family fortune he became the terror of the north of England. Like most bullies he liked 'soft' targets and often robbed monasteries and convents. In the end he was cornered in Yorkshire by the Sheriff and 600 men. They called on Denville to give himself up. What happened next?

2 The church was no better. The monasteries owned large areas of land and rented it out. Then they employed tough gangs to collect the rent from poor peasant farmers. In 1317 a gang grabbed a traveller on the path to a monastery and held him to ransom for £200. What was unusual about this gang?

3 A Scottish priest sacrificed a man at a black magic ceremony. He had his hands and feet cut off and his eyes put out as a punishment. Kind King David of Scotland took pity on the priest and gave him shelter in his palace. In 1114 the priest thanked the king by murdering his young son – he used the iron fingers of his artificial hands to tear the child apart. David decided to tear the priest apart . . . how?

4 The de Folville brothers had a fine career in theft and ransom. But when Eustace de Folville joined the army to fight for the king he was pardoned of all his crimes.

Brother Richard was a priest. A law officer chased rich Richard till the pilfering priest ran into a church and claimed sanctuary. ('No one can touch me while I'm in the church building.') The officer ignored the sanctuary rules, dragged Richard out and beheaded him. How was the officer rewarded for his success?

5 Sir Roger Swynnerton of Staffordshire was accused of murder. There were several witnesses who said they had seen him do it. Sir Roger was set free to return to Swynnerton village where the murder had taken place. What did Sir Roger do?

6 Henry II became fed up with his Archbishop of Canterbury, Thomas à Becket, and said that he wished he were rid of him. Four knights thought they'd do Henry a favour and get rid of Becket for him. They battered Becket to death as he clutched at his altar. Henry was horrified and felt it was his fault. As a punishment he went to the scene of the murder, walked barefoot into the Cathedral and prayed. There were several monks and priests there. How did they complete the punishment of the king?

Answers:

1 Deadly Denville's gang killed 200 before they were finally overcome.

2 The gang members were all monks! But don't be too surprised – in the 15th century there were records of parsons being arrested for poaching, highway robbery and forging coins. They also had a bad name for gambling and drinking in the local taverns. Two priests were arrested in 1453 for beating up an Oxford man – they were helped in the attack by a measly schoolteacher!

3 A wild horse was tied to each arm and leg, then they were sent off in different directions. Your local riding school will probably not allow you to try this on your teacher . . . but in the name of historical research, it's worth asking, I suppose.

WELL, AT LEAST IT'S A GOOD EXERCISE IN PHYSICS

4 The officer had broken sanctuary rules and killed a priest. The officer was punished by being beaten with rods outside all of the churches in the area!

5 The murderer was so upset by the witnesses that he forced them to pay him 50 marks as a punishment for speaking out against him.

6 They stripped him to the waist and took it in turn to give him three to five lashes from each of them. (That's more lashes than you have on your eyes!)

Painful punishments

Henry II tried to make modern laws but the punishments for breaking them were still very old-fashioned and definitely measly.

> **The Forger**
> Name — John Stubbs
> Crime — He did make copies of the king's coins and used the forged coins to buy food
> Punishment — John Stubbs's hand was tied to a block of wood. A meat axe was placed on his wrist and struck with a hammer till the hand was cut off
> [Amputation of a hand was a rare punishment but the law was still in force in 1820]

> **The Thief**
> Name — Peter of Clarendon
> Crime — Felony. He did steal a horse to the value of two shillings
> Punishment — The Sheriff of Wiltshire had a pit dug and filled with water which was then blessed by a priest. The thief was thrown in. If he sank he was innocent. Peter of Clarendon floated and was therefore guilty. He was taken out and executed.
> [Sheriff Ranulf Glanville of Yorkshire killed 120 men in this way]

> **The Beggar**
> Name — Martin of Cheapside
> Crime — Begging for money when fit and able for work
> Punishment — Three days and three nights in the stocks in the market place, fed only on bread and water. He was then thrown out of the town and ordered not to return
> [The kind Tudors reduced this punishment to one day and one night in the stocks in 1504]

The Attacker
Name — Thomas of Elderfield
Crime — Fought against George of Northway and did wound him
Punishment — Sentenced to fight a duel with George. He was defeated and the law demanded that Thomas's eyes be gouged out by George's Family. [It is recorded that Thomas was nursed back to health by St Wulfstan. His eyes were miraculously restored]

The Assassin
Name — The Earl of Athol
Crime — Assassinated King James I of Scotland in 1437
Punishment — Taken to the Cross in Edinburgh where he was crowned with a red-hot iron crown and his flesh was nipped off with red-hot pincers.

The Liar
Name — John de Hackford
Crime — In 1364 he announced that 10,000 men were gathering to murder the London councillors. This caused widespread fear and panic.
Punishment — He was jailed for a year. Every three months he was taken out, stood in a pillory (or Stretch-neck) with a stone round his neck and a notice "False Liar" pinned to his chest

The Hawk Finder
Name — John of Rivers
Crime — He did find his lordship's hawk on the roof of his house. He failed to report this to his lordship
Punishment — The hawk shall be fed on six ounces of flesh cut from John of Rivers' chest.

> **The Scold**
> Name – Ann Runcorn
> Crime – She did disgrace her husband by scolding him in public, calling him "villain" and "rogue".
> Punishment – Ann was fitted with a cage over her head called a "brank". A metal rod poked into her mouth to hold down her tongue. Ann had to sit on a horse facing backwards, and be led through the market where people could mock her.
> [A Brank in the town of Shrewsbury was last used in 1846]

Hawking Henry

A hawk was valued more than a peasant by the lords who owned it. A 14th-century historian told a story about Henry II's nasty habit – swearing – and how God taught him a bit of a lesson...

> In the early days of his reign Henry cast off his best falcon at a heron. The heron circled higher and higher, but the swift hawk had almost overtaken him when Henry cried out loud, 'By God's eyes or by God's gorge, that heron shall not escape – not even if God himself has decided it!' At these words the heron turned and as if by a miracle stuck his beak into the falcon's head and dashed out his brains. The heron, himself unhurt, threw the dying bird to the earth at the very feet of King Henry.

Wonder why God killed the hawk and not the offensive Henry?

Jolly John

The first Angevins were just like the first Normans. Father (Henry II) fought against sons Richard I, Geoffrey and Henry. But this time the boys had their mother, Eleanor, on their side. (Henry II tamed her treachery by locking her away for 16 years!)

Henry's favourite son was young John. When Henry found that John had joined his three brothers it broke the old king's heart. He died.

Richard took the throne. (His heart was a lion heart so it was harder to break.) Of course, Richard went off Crusading and got himself captured. John looked after the country, spent the royal money and made plans to pinch Richard's throne.

Richard forgave John ('You are just a child,' he said), then very kindly went off to another battle and got himself killed. John was king! But one of the measliest monarchs of the Middle Ages. He liked fine clothes, fine food, fine girlfriends . . . and he enjoyed upsetting people . . .

- John laughed at the long beards and national dress of the Irish princes – the Irish chieftains were upset.
- John married his cousin; the Archbishop of Canterbury objected but John got the Pope to overrule him – the Archbishop of Canterbury was upset.
- John arranged for the murder of his greatest rival, Arthur of Brittany in France – the French king (Philip II) was upset and went to war (though Arthur was too dead to be upset).
- John picked a new Archbishop of Canterbury against

the wishes of the Pope – the Pope was upset.
- John raised huge taxes from the English people and the barons to fight against France; the war went badly and the barons were upset. This, of course, led to . . .

The Magnet Carter
The Barons made John agree to give power back to them and the people; no taxes, no wars and no laws unless the people agreed . . .

Please note that this is utter nonsense of the kind you would only find in a Horrible History. Any boring teacher will tell you that Magna Carta means 'Great Charter' in Latin.

John died after pigging himself on peaches and cider. But the food in the Middle Ages was so bad he could have died just as easily from drinking a glass of water!

Foul food

In the Middle Ages the Church had rules about what you could (or could not) eat. Until the start of the 13th century adults were 'forbidden four-footed flesh-meat'. (Try saying that with a mouthful of mushy peas.) And no one was allowed meat on a Friday – only fish.

The trouble was, people cheated. If they couldn't eat 'four-footed flesh' then they ate large birds. Turkeys hadn't been discovered so they ate birds called bustards. What happened? Bustards became extinct in England!

Fancy a bit of red meat on a Friday? Then eat a beaver. Beavers used their tails for swimming, so they could be called fish ... couldn't they? (Er ... no, actually.) What happened? Beavers became extinct in Britain.

And it wasn't only bustards and beavers that had a hard time. A 1393 French recipe book advised eating hedgehog – skinned, cleaned and roasted like a chicken. Of course, catching hedgehogs was harder in those days. You didn't usually find them ready-squashed in the middle of the road. Or perhaps you did!

LOOK! MEALS ON WHEELS!

Tasty treats

It wasn't only turkey that was unknown to the Middle Age munchers. There were no potatoes either. Imagine a world with no chips or crisps!

Of course, they had the dreaded cabbage. But forget school-dinner cabbage – pale grey strips of slime flavoured with sweaty socks. Try this recipe for cabbage soup and see if the Middle Ages people had more scrumptious scran than you . . .

Cabbage soup

You need:
- 600g cabbage (leaves cut into strips)
- 225g onions (peeled and chopped small)
- 225g leeks (white part sliced into thin rings)
- half-teaspoon of salt
- quarter teaspoon of coriander
- quarter teaspoon of cinnamon
- quarter teaspoon of sugar
- quarter teaspoon of saffron strands (rather expensive – can be missed out, or use half a teaspoon of turmeric powder)
- 850 ml water
- chicken stock-cube (or vegetable stock-cube if you're a vegetarian)

Method:
1. Boil the water in a saucepan and crumble in the stock cube
2. Stir in the saffron, cinnamon, coriander, salt and sugar
3. Add the sliced cabbage, chopped onion and leek rings to the boiling stock
4. Cover the saucepan and boil gently for 20 minutes
5. Serve with 1cm squares of toast or small strips of fried bacon on top

The only difference in the original recipe was that it said, 'Boil the cabbages all morning'. But cabbages in the Middle Ages were tougher and needed it. Boil modern cabbages all morning and you'll end up with school-dinner green slime.

When it came to sweet dishes the rich people ate all the sugar they could get their teeth on... until the sugar rotted their teeth, of course. One flavour that was popular then is rare now – the flavour of roses.

Try this rose pudding and see what you think. (Cooks in the Middle Ages didn't have liquidizers, of course, but you might. Cheat a bit and use one if you have. Any greenfly you've failed to wash off the rose petals will be turned into serious hospital cases.)

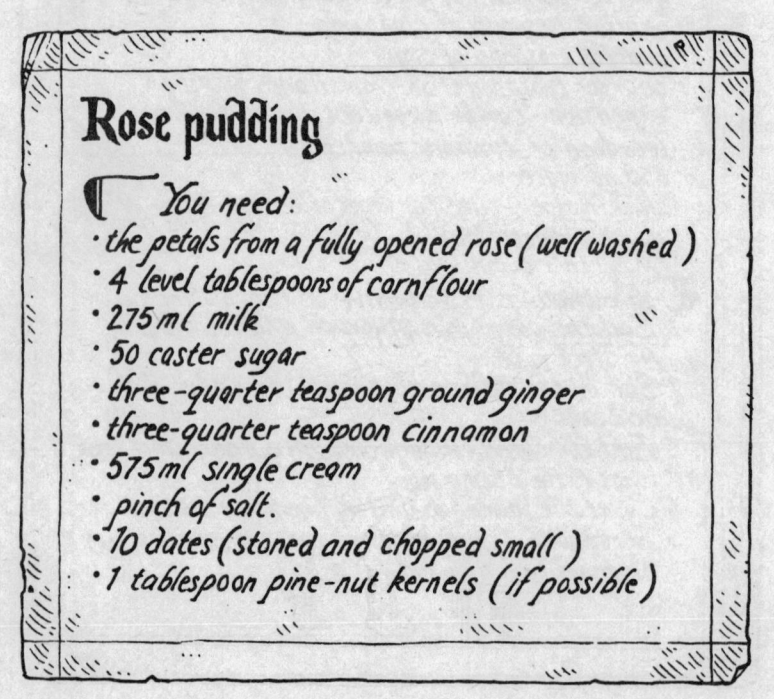

Rose pudding

You need:
- the petals from a fully opened rose (well washed)
- 4 level tablespoons of cornflour
- 275 ml milk
- 50 caster sugar
- three-quarter teaspoon ground ginger
- three-quarter teaspoon cinnamon
- 575 ml single cream
- pinch of salt
- 10 dates (stoned and chopped small)
- 1 tablespoon pine-nut kernels (if possible)

Method:

1. Boil the rose petals in water for two minutes
2. Press the petals between kitchen towels under a heavy weight
3. Put the cornflour in a saucepan and slowly add the milk, stirring all the time
4. Put the pan on to heat and warm until the mixture starts to thicken
5. Pour the mixture into a blender, add sugar, cinnamon, ginger and rose petals
6. Blend until smooth (or until the greenfly have a headache)
7. Blend in cream and salt then return the mixture to the saucepan
8. Heat and stir until the mixture is like thick cream
9. Stir in dates and pine-nut kernels and heat for further two minutes
10. Pour into glasses and leave to cool (stirring to stop a skin forming)
11. Eat this straight from the fridge and amaze your parents... just don't tell them that you pinched a prize rose from the garden

Boozing bachelors

In the Middle Ages everyone drank ale. It was safer than drinking the water in some of the filthy large towns.

Special ales were brewed for special occasions and usually *sold* to drinkers (you'd expect to get your drinks free today). So, a man would brew a 'Bride Ale' when he got married. The wedding guests all bought pots of the ale and the money went to the bride.

Imagine going to a wedding today being told, 'Raise your glasses of champagne and drink a toast to the bride – but don't forget to drop a fiver in the best man's hat!' A measly marriage if ever there was one!

Funerals were another popular occasion for a special brew. The corpse often paid for the special ale . . . usually before he died. This was especially popular with drinkers who liked their ale with a bit of body.

The Church became upset by all this drinking and tried to ban it. People enjoyed themselves too much so the Church decided, 'If you can't beat them, join them.' They brewed 'Churchyard Ales' and sold them to raise money for repairs to church buildings!

The Lord of the manor brewed an ale about three times a year; he expected his workers to buy it at a high price. It was a sort of extra tax the workers had to pay. But sometimes the bachelors of the village were given a challenging treat.

They could drink as much of the ale as they wanted, free . . . so long as they stayed on their feet. If they sat down they had to pay.

Foul food facts
1 Butchers were banned from slaughtering animals in the City of London. They'd been in the habit of dumping the guts on the pavement outside the Grey Friars' monastery. A Winchester butcher killed a cow on the pavement outside his shop, while 15th-century Coventry cooks threw chicken guts out of their kitchen windows into the street.
2 Butchers were not allowed to sell meat by candlelight. This was so the customer could see what they were getting! A man was caught trying to sell pork from a dead pig he'd found in a ditch. He was fastened in the pillory and the rotten meat burned under his nose – a common punishment for this sort of fraud.
3 Large towns had takeaway food suppliers selling delicious thrushes (at two for a penny) and tasty hot sheep's feet. They would even deliver cooked food to your home. (Could the sheep's feet maybe deliver themselves . . . simply stroll round to the customer's house?)
4 If you went to a tavern for a mug of ale you could have 'Huffcap', 'Angel's Food', 'Dragon's Milk' or 'Mad Dog Ale' (*that* had a bit of a bite to it). These were probably safer than Eleanor Rummyng's ale – she allowed her hens to

roost over the brewing vats. Their droppings fell into the ale and old Eleanor just stirred them in before she sold it.

5 Drinks could be pretty nasty with lots of 'foreign bodies' floating in them. One 13th-century writer complained that some ale was as thick as soup. 'You didn't drink it, you filtered it through your teeth.' (Of course, King Edward IV had his brother, Clarence, drowned in a barrel of wine in 1478. Now that's what you'd call a foreign body in your drink!)

6 Many towns checked the quality of bread and punished bakers who tried to cheat. Some were found guilty of adding sand to loaves and, in one disgusting case, a loaf contained cobwebs.

7 Housewives often prepared dough then took it to a baker to be cooked. Some bakers had a clever trick. They placed the housewife's dough on the counter. There was a small trapdoor in this counter with a boy underneath. While the baker kept the woman chatting, the boy opened the trapdoor and pinched a fistful of dough. The measly baker made the stolen dough into loaves which he baked and sold. The housewife paid him for baking her loaf and went home with less than she'd brought. (If he was caught then he spent a day in the pillory – there are no records of the boy-thief being caught and punished.)

8 Servants were forbidden to wear hanging sleeves like their masters. This was partly because lords hated their servants to look too grand . . . and partly because long sleeves dropped into the soup as they served it!

9 Henry VIII is famous for his Terrible Tudor feasts but in 1467 there were feasts just as fattening as those. Richard, Earl of Warwick, threw a little party to celebrate his brother becoming Archbishop of York. The 60 cooks prepared 104 oxen, 2,000 pigs, 1,000 sheep and 13,000 sweet dishes. In case this made the feasters thirsty there were 300 large barrels of ale and 100 casks of wine.

10 Peasants ate bacon because it was easy to kill and salt a pig every winter. They ate vegetables because they could grow those themselves. As a result most noblemen would never be seen eating bacon or vegetables!

Mucky manners

Young people had books to teach them table manners. Unfortunately not a lot of young people could read. It may have been better to have had illustrations to help.

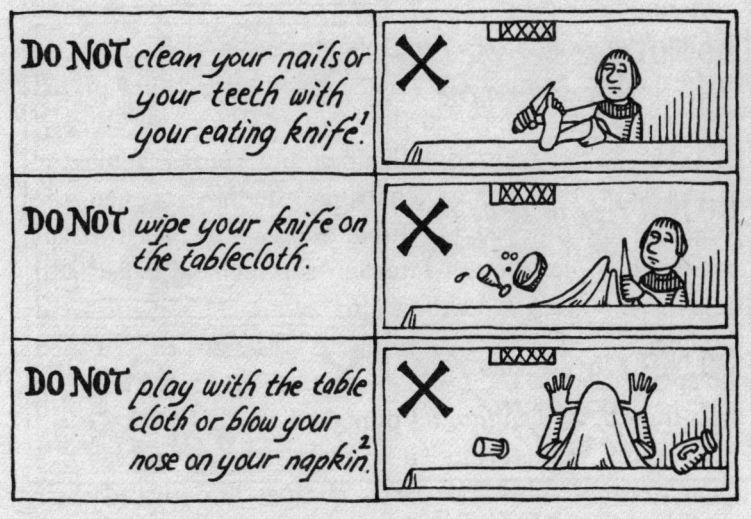

DO NOT clean your nails or your teeth with your eating knife.[1]	✗
DO NOT wipe your knife on the tablecloth.	✗
DO NOT play with the tablecloth or blow your nose on your napkin.[2]	✗

1. Scratching your head at the table 'as if clawing at a flea' was also impolite.
2. But it was common for people to pick their noses at the table.

DO NOT *dip your bread in the soup.*	✗
DO NOT *fill your soup spoon too full or blow on your soup.*	✗
DO NOT *eat noisily or clean your bowl by licking it out.*	✗
DO NOT *speak while your mouth is full of food.*[1]	✗
DO NOT *spit over the table but spit on the floor.*	✗
DO NOT *tear at meat but cut it with a knife first.*	✗
DO NOT *take the best food for yourself. Share it.*[2]	✗

1. You could burp at the table... but not too close to someone's face.
2. And you are asked not to steal food from someone else's plate.

Terrible toilets
The Middle Ages were pretty smelly times. Most rubbish ended in the streets. Butchers killed an animal, sold the meat and then threw the guts into the street. The town councils passed the odd law to clean up the streets and London had public conveniences built over the river Fleet to the west of the city.

One writer said that 'each toilet seat is filled with a buttock' so the boatmen sailing underneath had to watch out!

> SO FAR THIS WEEK I'VE HIT THREE ROWING BOATS AND A BARGE

And it wasn't only the boatmen who had this problem. Many private toilets took a bit of controlling. The London council took Thomas Wytte and William Hockele to court in 1321 . . .

A jury decided that Ebbgate Lane used to be a right of way for all men until it was closed up by Wytte and Hockele who built toilets. These toilets projected from the walls of the houses so that human filth falls on to the heads of the passers-by.

Not everyone bothered with a toilet. They shared a room with animals and behaved like the animals. Even by 1515 a

Dutchman was complaining about the filthy English homes...

> *The floors are commonly of clay, strewed with rushes under which lies undisturbed an ancient collection of beer, spittle, grease, bones, droppings of animals and men and everything that is nasty.*

Of course, careful housewives collected the family urine because it helped with the laundry! They made their own soap by boiling wood ash with scraps of meat fat. The urine was stored until it was really strong and then added to the wash where it acted as a sort of bleach. (Note: If you fancy bleaching your hair then go to the chemist for the bleach. It will cost a bit more but at least you won't smell like a broken toilet.)

Lousy Lancastrians

The last Angevin king was Richard II. He was a poor weak thing and no one was too upset when his cousin Henry had him thrown off the throne in 1399. Henry Lancaster became Henry IV. He had so many lice on his head they reckoned his hair wouldn't grow. He was lousy . . . the first of several lousy Lancastrian kings.

The trouble is his grandson, Henry VI, was another measly weak king. And weak kings were just asking for strong lords to fight for their throne. When Henry VI went mad in 1453 his Lancaster family started scrapping with the York family for power.

Each family had a rose for a badge – a red rose for Lancaster, a white rose for York. After 30 years of bloody battles, Henry 'Red Rose' Tudor defeated Richard 'White Rose' III but, cleverly, married Elizabeth 'White Rose' York. This brought the fighting to an end. Those battles became known as 'The Wars of the Roses'.

The Middle Ages began and ended with important battles . . . and there were several others in between. If those battles had been won by the losers then history would have changed.

Bloody battles

Nowadays wars are fought between machines – laser-guided missiles, tanks, submarines, bombs and aeroplanes. A fighting man can kill a million people at the push of a button and never set eyes on one of his victims.

But in the Middle Ages men fought hand to hand – or at least within arrow-shot of the enemy. There was plenty of blood, plenty of cruelty and lots of stupidity.

But in the excitement of a battle it's easy to make mistakes. Winning (or losing) was often decided by simple decisions. How would history have changed if you'd been in command? What would you have done in these famous battles of the measly Middle Ages?

1 Hastings, 14 October, 1066
Armies:
King Harold of England v. Duke William of Normandy. The first major battle in the Norman Conquest.
Battle:
- 9:00 a.m. Harold's English army are sitting on Senlac Hill, tired but happy to defend the place.
- The Normans have three lines of attack – archers, followed by foot-soldiers followed by knights on horseback.
- The first Norman attack fails – the archers are firing uphill and the English catch the arrows easily on their shields.
- The foot-soldiers advance but the English drive them back with spears and stones (but very few archers).
- The Normans turn and stumble back down the hill. Harold turns to you and asks, 'What do we do now?'

What do you tell him?

Advice:

> FOLLOW THEM DOWN THE HILL AND KILL THEM AS THEY RUN AWAY. THEIR FOOT SOLDIERS ARE BUMPING INTO THEIR OWN KNIGHTS. THEIR ARCHERS HAVE USED UP ALL THEIR ARROWS. IT'S CHAOS. WE'LL SLAUGHTER THEM!

> STAY AT THE TOP OF THE HILL. LET THEM ATTACK AS OFTEN AS THEY LIKE, THEY'LL WEAR THEMSELVES OUT IN THE END. OUR MEN ARE TOO TIRED TO RUN AFTER THEM THEN START KILLING. WE'VE HAD HARDLY ANY REST FOR WEEKS

2 Bannockburn, near Stirling, Scotland, 24 June, 1314

Armies:

Edward II of England v. Robert the Bruce of Scotland. Battle in Scottish war of independence against England.

Battle:

- Robert Bruce's 40,000 Scots are besieging the English in Stirling so Edward marches 60,000 English soldiers to drive them off.
- When the English draw close to Stirling they see the Scots camped on the far side of a swampy stream, the Bannock Burn.
- The Scottish foot-soldiers are armed with long poles with axe heads and spikes on the end – weapons called pikes.
- They group themselves tightly so that charging knights

will face a hedgehog of metal bristles.
- Edward's 2000 knights want to charge at the pikes, but first they have to tear doors off nearby cottages to make a wooden path across the swamp.

What would you advise Edward to do?

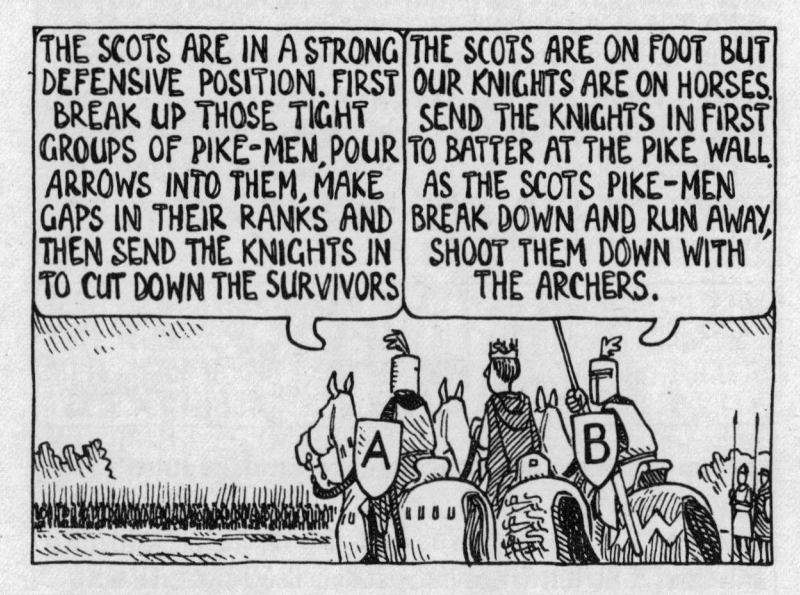

> THE SCOTS ARE IN A STRONG DEFENSIVE POSITION. FIRST BREAK UP THOSE TIGHT GROUPS OF PIKE-MEN, POUR ARROWS INTO THEM, MAKE GAPS IN THEIR RANKS AND THEN SEND THE KNIGHTS IN TO CUT DOWN THE SURVIVORS

> THE SCOTS ARE ON FOOT BUT OUR KNIGHTS ARE ON HORSES. SEND THE KNIGHTS IN FIRST TO BATTER AT THE PIKE WALL. AS THE SCOTS PIKE-MEN BREAK DOWN AND RUN AWAY, SHOOT THEM DOWN WITH THE ARCHERS.

3 Crécy, Northern France, 26 August, 1346
Armies:
Edward III of England v. Philip VI of France. The first major battle in the Hundred Years War.
Battle:
- Edward's army of 18,000 has less than 4000 armoured knights. He faces Philip's 38,000 men including 12,000 knights.
- The English wait on a small hill. The French have to cross a stream and attack uphill (but this will be no problem for the knights.)

- As the two armies face one another there is a shower of rain. The English take the strings off their longbows and keep them dry. The French archers use crossbows and the soaked string makes them pretty useless.
- The sun comes out and it is straight in the eyes of the French. They can't make out the enemy forces very clearly. They can see that the English archers are at the front.
- Behind the archers the English knights are waiting on foot. The English knights cannot reach their horses in time to fight off the French knights!

What do you advise Philip to do?

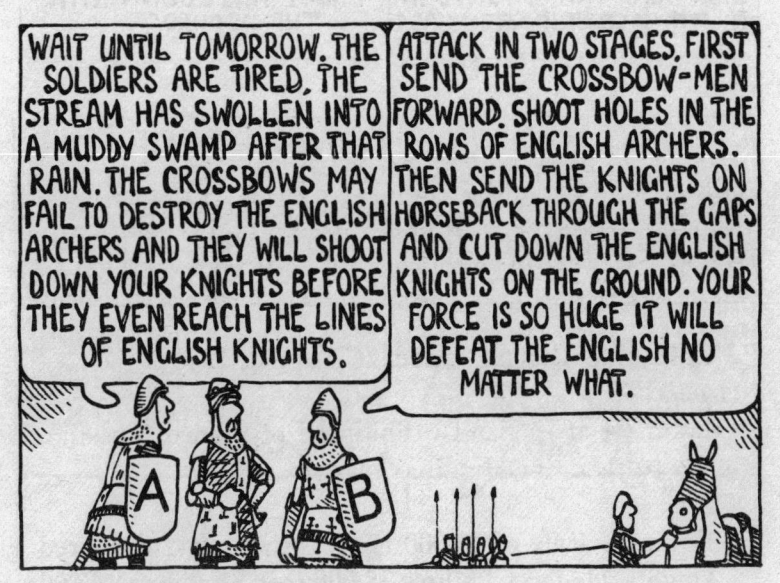

> **A:** WAIT UNTIL TOMORROW. THE SOLDIERS ARE TIRED. THE STREAM HAS SWOLLEN INTO A MUDDY SWAMP AFTER THAT RAIN. THE CROSSBOWS MAY FAIL TO DESTROY THE ENGLISH ARCHERS AND THEY WILL SHOOT DOWN YOUR KNIGHTS BEFORE THEY EVEN REACH THE LINES OF ENGLISH KNIGHTS.

> **B:** ATTACK IN TWO STAGES. FIRST SEND THE CROSSBOW-MEN FORWARD. SHOOT HOLES IN THE ROWS OF ENGLISH ARCHERS. THEN SEND THE KNIGHTS ON HORSEBACK THROUGH THE GAPS AND CUT DOWN THE ENGLISH KNIGHTS ON THE GROUND. YOUR FORCE IS SO HUGE IT WILL DEFEAT THE ENGLISH NO MATTER WHAT.

4 Bosworth Field, Leicester, England, 22 August, 1485
Armies:
King Richard III and the Yorkists v. Henry Tudor and the Lancastrians. The final battle in the Wars of the Roses.

Battle:
- Richard has won the race to get his army on higher ground; he has reached the top of Ambion Hill and waits.
- Henry's army had trouble lining up on the rough ground at the foot of the hill.
- Richard could charge at them while they sort themselves out, but he has a couple of problems: a) A third army is waiting nearby under the command of Lord Stanley. Stanley promised to fight for Richard . . . and Stanley promised to fight for Henry Tudor! b) Richard is unsure about one of his own commanders, Northumberland, who is at his back.

What do you advise Richard III to do?

> WAIT. SEE WHICH WAY STANLEY'S ARMY FIGHTS. IF YOU CHARGE DOWN THE HILL NOW YOU MAY DEFEAT HENRY TUDOR... BUT STANLEY COULD THEN ATTACK YOU WITH FRESH MEN. LET HENRY TUDOR'S MEN EXHAUST THEMSELVES ATTACKING UP THE HILL AT YOU.

> CHARGE. IF YOU CUT DOWN HENRY TUDOR'S ARMY THEN STANLEY WILL KNOW THAT HE HAS TO FIGHT WITH YOU. SIMILARLY, NORTHUMBERLAND WILL SUPPORT YOU WHEN HE SEES YOU ARE THE WINNING SIDE. DON'T GIVE HENRY TUDOR'S ARMY TIME TO SORT THEMSELVES OUT!

Answers:
1 Hastings Harold follows the advice from soldier 'A' . . . and loses. Once the English leave the hill the Normans turn and attack them on the flat ground. (Some historians believe the 'running away' was just a trick to get the English off the high ground.) It works. Norman archers draw fresh supplies of arrows and fire high in the air. As the English hold their shields over their heads the Norman knights charge them from the front. Harold should have listened to soldier 'B' and stayed where he was. He is wounded with an arrow in the eye then cut down by Norman knights. The Normans will go on to rule England.

2 Bannockburn Edward follows advice from soldier 'B' . . . and loses. The knights feel they are the most important soldiers there and they want the glory of charging at Robert's army first. The archers are hardly used. The knights struggle to cross the swampy ground and then find the Scots have dug pits and traps for the horses. There is no great charge but English knights stumble into Scottish pikes where they are cut down and driven back to drown in the swampy stream. Edward II runs away and his army runs after him. The Scottish people are free of the English.

3 Crécy Philip follows advice 'B' . . . and loses. The crossbow-men fire . . . and are met by deadly showers of arrows from the English longbows. They stumble back . . . and are trampled by their own knights moving forward. The powerful longbows punch holes in the French armour. Horses and knights fall, more horses and knights stumble over them. When a few knights do get through they are surrounded and pulled down by the English knights on foot. Ten thousand French fighters die, and King Philip is wounded by an arrow in the neck but escapes with his life. The English king can claim to be King of France.

4 Bosworth Field Richard follows advice from soldier 'A' . . . and loses. He misses his chance to hit Henry Tudor's army at their weakest. Henry Tudor's men use cannon and arrows to damage Richard on his hilltop. Richard's men come down from their hilltop and fight hand to hand with Henry's men. When Richard calls for Northumberland to move forward with fresh forces, Northumberland refuses. Richard leads a charge personally at Henry Tudor but Stanley decides this is the moment to join the battle – on Henry Tudor's side. Richard is cut down – the second and last English King to die in battle – and Henry Tudor takes the crown. This is the end of the Wars of the Roses. For many historians this is the end of the Middle Ages.

Did you know . . . ?

The Duke of Suffolk had been a loyal servant to Lancastrian king, Henry VI. But when he lost in battle to the French he had to go. Henry didn't want to execute his faithful friend so he sent him off into exile. The Duke of Suffolk set sail from Ipswich but didn't get very far. At Dover his enemies caught up with him, dragged him into a small boat and cut his head off with a rusty sword. (WARNING: Do *not* try this in your local park pond. Cutting someone's head off with a rusty sword could give them a serious case of blood poisoning.)

Sickly singers
Not everyone was horrified by war. Some enjoyed the excitement. Bertrand de Born was a troubadour – a sort of Middle Ages pop-singer. One of his biggest hits was this gory little number . . .

> *My heart swells up with happiness every time I see*
> *A mighty castle being attacked, its strong walls beaten down,*
> *The soldiers on those broken walls being struck down to the ground,*
> *While horses of the dead and fallen roam the field at random.*
> *And, when battle starts to seethe, let all you noble men*
> *Put all your will to breaking heads and arms.*
> *It's better far for you to die in battle than to lose and live.*
> *I tell you that my greatest joy is just to hear the shouts,*
> *'On! On!' from both sides and the screams of horses with no riders,*
> *And the groans of, 'Help me! Help me!' from the fallen wounded.*
> *The bliss when I see great and small fall in the ditches and the grass*

*And when I see the corpses pierced clean through by
   shafts of spears!*
*So, Knights, give up your castles, leave your lands or
   lose your cities,*
But my lords, I beg you, never ever give up war.

Woeful women

The Church in the Middle Ages taught that men were better than women. This could have something to do with the fact that the priests were men!

Women were told they had to obey their male relatives till they married, then they had to obey their husbands. Even in the 1990s women can still choose to get married with a promise to 'love, honour and obey' their husbands.

And, if the wife decided to disobey, then the husband was encouraged to beat her. He was told not to do this if he was drunk or in a temper. Just if she 'deserved' it. As an Italian proverb said . . .

> *A horse, whether good or bad, needs a spur. A woman, whether good or bad, needs a lord and master — and sometimes a stick.*

A priest, Robert d'Abrissel, went further when he said:

> *A woman is a witch, a snake, a plague, a rat, a rash, a poison, a burning flame and an assistant of the Devil.*

WHO ME?

Do you get the idea that he didn't like women very much? The trouble is men listened to him, believed him and treated women badly because of his wicked words.

Women were told it was sinful to use make-up, to dye their hair or pluck their eyebrows. The priests said this was 'vanity' and women would be punished in Hell. The women did these things anyway.

> IF I'M GOING TO HELL, I'LL WANT TO LOOK NICE WHEN I GET THERE

Then, in the 14th century, priests became worried that men were wearing colourful, fancy clothes and becoming more like those 'snaky, ratty, poisonous' women! And the worst thing a man could do was to be like a woman. That was a sin. So the measly Church started to frown upon ...

Foul fashions
Fashionable men gave up wearing gowns and started wearing tights. The really fashionable young men wore their tunics so short that a writer complained the tights revealed 'parts of the body that should be hidden'!

The friars, monks and priests had some savage things to say about fancy 14th-century fashions...

... and the women *did* burn their steeple hats – for a while. When measly monk Tom took himself off, the women went back to wearing their steeple hats which were ... taller than ever!

> AND FOR THE FEMININE FOOT WE HAVE PLATFORM SHOES

> "A DREADFUL WASTE OF CORK FOR THE SOLES AND EXTRA MATERIAL TO MAKE THE DRESSES REACH THE GROUND"
> 15th CENTURY CHURCH COMPLAINT

In many countries laws were passed in the Middle Ages saying that only nobles could wear fine clothes. Peasants were not to be seen wearing rich clothes – otherwise people would mistake them for someone better!

Most of the laws were there to control women's clothes. Laws were passed to stop women wearing platform shoes, for example. Generally men used any way they could to make sure women 'obeyed' them. As Goodman of Paris told his wife ...

> *Copy the behaviour of a dog which loves to obey its master; even if the master whips it, the dog follows, wagging its tail.*

> THEN BITES HIM

But, not surprisingly, women were not always as meek as Mr Goodman would have liked. Women had a difficult a life in the Middle Ages. But some fought back. A few were true . . .

Hooray heroines
Jeanne de Clisson

In 1313 Olivier de Clisson was executed on the orders of Philip the Fair, King of France. His wife, Jeanne, decided he was Philip the Un-fair and decided to get her own back. First she sold off all of her lands to raise money. Jeanne bought three warships; they were painted black and had red sails. Admiral Jeanne began destroying Philip's ships and murdering their crews . . . but she always left two or three alive to carry the story back to the king. After all, that was part of the fun!

Philip died – which could have spoilt Jeanne's fun – but she decided to continue her revenge on his sons as they took the French throne. After 13 bloody years the last son of Philip died and Jeanne retired. It was said that she enjoyed capturing ships with French noblemen on board, then personally chopping off their heads with her axe. (Some women with a fleet may have a fish and chip shop. But when Jeanne caught her enemies on a fishing ship then she would have a fishing-ship chop.)

Her grey ghost still walks the walls of Clisson Castle – don't go there if your name is Philip!

Marcia Ordelaffi
Marcia's husband, Francesco, was not an easy man to live with. In 1358 his son suggested that Francesco should surrender his fortress in Italy. Old Fran didn't like the idea much so he stabbed the lad to death.

The kid killer left wife Marcia in charge of the defence of Cesena a few years later. Sensible Marcia did NOT suggest that they should surrender . . . at least, not until he had gone off to defend another city.

Marcia suspected that one of her councillors was talking to the enemy about a surrender. She had him arrested and beheaded. This was quite a good way to make sure he didn't talk to anyone ever again.

Tough-talking Marcia then talked her way out of the siege and escaped alive with her family.

Madame de Montfort
When John de Montfort was captured in a 1341 battle in Brittany, his wife took over the war effort. Apart from raising armies she liked to do a bit of fighting herself. While her town of Hennebont was under siege she rode out in full armour to lead her soldiers. Arrows rained down but she rallied the men. She told the women of Hennebont to cut their skirts short; that way they could run up to the ramparts with stones and pots of boiling tar to pour over the attackers.

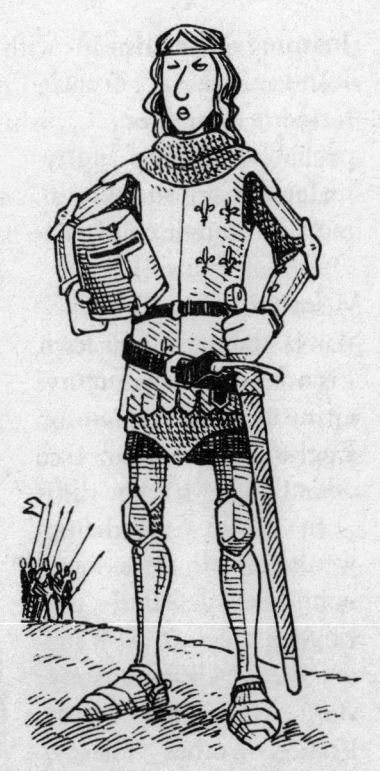

When the attackers grew tired Madame de Montfort led a group of knights out of the town through a secret gate. They rode round behind the enemy and destroyed half of the army. The siege was over and Hennebont was saved.

John de Montfort escaped and hurried home to his warrior wife. What did the wimp do next? Help her? Take over as army leader? Give her a thank-you kiss? No! He died! How very inconsiderate.

Madame de Montfort carried on the war for her son. She went mad, was captured by the English and locked away for 30 years till she died.

Jeanne la Pucelle
Jeanne was a French farmer's daughter . . . probably! (Some nutty historians say she was in fact the daughter of the Queen of France!)

Jeanne heard angel voices telling her to lead French soldiers to victory against the invading English. Against all the odds this is what she did.

In spite of being wounded with a crossbow bolt she defeated the English siege of Orléans in 1429. Unfortunately she couldn't defeat France's other enemy, Burgundy. The Burgundians captured Jeanne and very sensibly sold her to the English. The English couldn't execute her as a soldier, so they said she was a witch and burned her at the stake. Her main crime? Wearing men's clothes!

The English lost the war in the end – which served them right for being so mean and measly to this 20-year-old young woman. She became known as Joan of Arc.

Isabella of England
Isabella was the daughter of King Edward III and a useful bargaining tool for old Ed. At three years old she was

engaged to Pedro the Cruel of Spain – luckily for Isabella that one fell through! When she was 15, King Ed decided to marry her off to Count Louis de Male. Now King Ed had led the English at the battle of Crécy where Louis's dad had been killed. Louis said, 'No!' to the idea of marrying the English king's daughter.

His people locked him away until he agreed to marry Isabella. After a few months of prison he gave in and he was released from his prison. Louis was still closely guarded, of course, but they said 'he couldn't so much as pee without his guards knowing.' (Charming!) Just before the wedding Louis went out hawking and chased after a heron . . . and didn't stop till he was over the border in France! He'd escaped . . . and Isabella was ditched.

But Isabella was a tough lady. Four years later she promised to marry another young man, Berard d'Albret. Just as she was about to set sail for the wedding in France she changed her mind and went home.

She'd made a monkey out of Berard. Or, rather, she made a monk out of him. Poor Berard was so upset he gave up women altogether and joined a monastery.

91

Did you know . . . ?
In the 14th century, Emperor Ludwig's daughter was married . . . but it was Ludwig who said, 'I will.' Why? Because his daughter was too young to talk. When she grew up dumb, people said, 'It's God's way of showing that Ludwig shouldn't have married off his baby daughter.' But why did the girl have to suffer? Why didn't God strike Ludwig dumb?

Cheerless children

If women had a hard time then how did children manage? Would you have survived to your present age? Probably not! Look at how the Middle Ages were...

Kruel for kids

1 Parents paid little attention to children till they were five or six. After all, they were probably going to die. Only one child in three lived to their first birthday. Only one in ten lived to their tenth. (No one made birthday-cake candles in those days. There wasn't enough business!)

2 Parents of the Middle Ages may have been measly, but at least they were a small improvement on Anglo-Saxon parents. Many of the Anglo-Saxons believed that a child born on a Friday would have a miserable life – so they spared them the unhappiness by killing them when they were born! Others 'tested' the new baby by putting it in a dangerous place – a roof-top or a tree branch. If it cried it was a wimp and was killed – if it laughed it lived. (And if it laughed so hard it fell out of the tree it died anyway!)

3 But life was still very tough for children in the Middle Ages. If the plague didn't get you then one of the other Middle Age marauders might! In 1322 Bernard de Irlaunde's baby daughter was playing in her father's shop. A passing pig wandered into the shop, bit the baby on the head and killed her. What a swine!

4 Children from rich families were cared for by nurses. The babies were wrapped in tight bands of cloth so they couldn't move – this was supposed to make their legs grow straight. In fact the lack of use made them weak for a year or two.

PERHAPS THAT'S TOO TIGHT!

5 Peasant children, on the other hand, had no clothes at all until they could walk. Before then they were kept warm by being laid in front of the fire. Curious little crawlers ended up cooked! But even the ones who lay still could have an accident. An old law said . . .

If a woman place her infant by the hearth and a man put water in the cauldron and it boileth over, and the child be scalded to death, the woman must be punished for her neglect.

If there was a law against it then there must have been a lot of cases of it happening. (Notice it's the woman who gets the blame and not the man? But that's another story!)

6 Parents didn't have the Royal Society for the Prevention of Accidents to advise them! They could be very careless about where they left their children. In Canterbury some very young children were left by the river and drowned. In another case an archer was practising his shooting and accidentally shot a child.

GO ON, I DARE YA

7 Worst of all were the beggars who broke their children's limbs so the public would give generously to the twisted, suffering little child!

8 Writers suggested that it was a mistake for parents to be too kind to their children. Children should be respectful to parents. One boy told how he would greet his father with the words . . .

> *My right reverent and worshipful father, I praise your good fatherhood in the most humble way possible and humbly beg your good fatherhood for your daily blessing.*

GOOD BOY, NOW HELP ME WITH THIS CAULDRON OF BOILING WATER

(This may well be a wise thing to say to your own father if you are planning to ask for an increase in pocket money.)
9 Don't laugh, girls. It would have been worse still for you. A book on a girl's behaviour said she mustn't laugh too loud, swear, walk too fast, yawn too wide or jerk her shoulders around. The advice on dealing with troublesome girls went . . .

> If your daughters will rebel
> and not bow down low,
> If any of them do some wrong
> then do not curse and blow.
> Just take a large rod in your
> hand and beat them in a row
> Until they cry for mercy and
> until their guilt they know.

This comes from the late-Middle Ages poem, 'How the Good Wife Taught Her Daughter', which was written by . . . a man, of course!
10 Boys who served lords had to stand perfectly still in the

castle hall while their masters ate. A 15th-century book said...

> Take no seat but be ready to stand until you are told to sit down. Keep your hands and feet still. Do not scratch yourself or lean against a post while your master is present. Bow low and answer your lord when he speaks to you, otherwise stand as still as a stone until he speaks to you.

Sounds a bit like school assemblies today. And, talking about schools...

Schools – the good news
- You didn't have to go if you were poor... or a girl.
- Most boys only went to school from the ages of 7 to 14.
- There was no homework.
- There were no spelling corrections – you spelled English any way you wanted to.

Schools – the bad news
- You had no break-times – only a short stop for lunch.
- Make a mistake and you were beaten – usually with branches of a birch tree.
- You had to buy your own paper, ink and books – which were very expensive.
- And of course there were 'School Rules'...

School rules . . . OK?
Westminster School in the 13th century had the following rules . . .

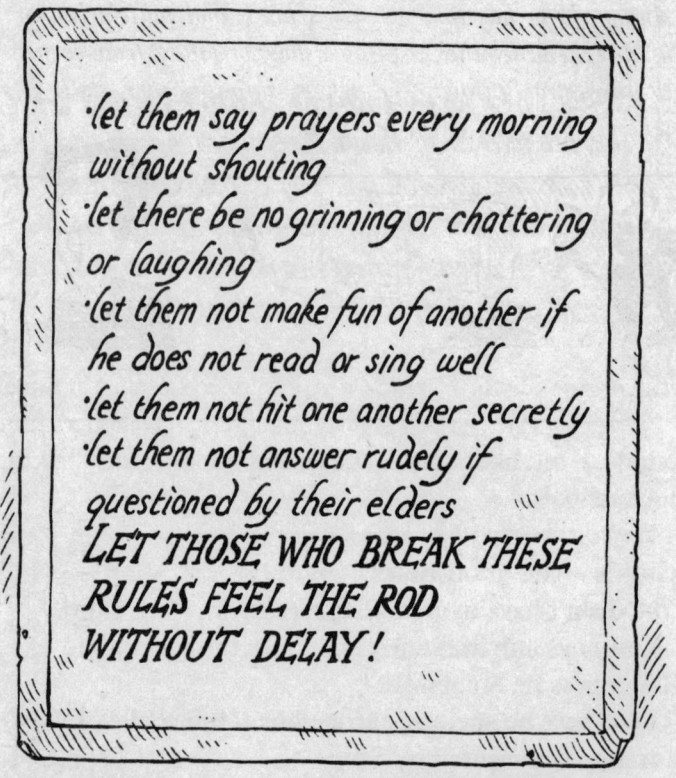

> • let them say prayers every morning without shouting
> • let there be no grinning or chattering or laughing
> • let them not make fun of another if he does not read or sing well
> • let them not hit one another secretly
> • let them not answer rudely if questioned by their elders
> LET THOSE WHO BREAK THESE RULES FEEL THE ROD WITHOUT DELAY!

Not too bad so far? Not much different from your own school, apart from the bit about being hit with a rod!

But if you knew Latin then you *had* to speak it. For each word of English or French that you spoke you received a stroke of the rod. Just imagine, turning to your friend and saying, 'Please can I borrow your book?' would get you six of the best. Measly!

And some of the other rules are odd. But they must have

needed these rules because someone actually did these dreadful deeds . . .

> *Anyone who has torn to pieces his school mate's bed or hidden the bedclothes or thrown shoes or pillow from corner to corner or thrown the school into disorder shall be severely punished in the morning.*

No wonder this boy's 15th-century poem was so popular with pupils. He wrote about being late for school and giving a cheeky reply to his teacher . . .

My master looks like he is mad
'Where have you been, my sorry lad?'
'Milking ducks my mother had!'
It is no wonder that I'm sad.

My master peppered my backside with speed,
It was worse than fennel seed;
He would not stop till it did bleed,
I'm truly sorry for his deed.

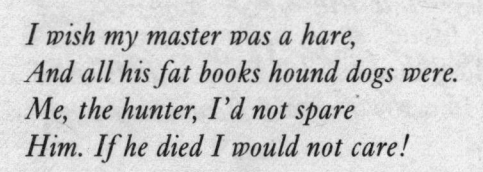

I wish my master was a hare,
And all his fat books hound dogs were.
Me, the hunter, I'd not spare
Him. If he died I would not care!

Why was the boy late? You might well ask. Well, school often began at five o'clock in the morning in summer time! Wouldn't you be late?

Schools – the bad news for teachers

- Schoolteachers were not very well paid. Two hungry Huntingdon teachers were arrested for poaching in 1225.
- In 1381 a Suffolk teacher was arrested for riotous behaviour – if he was anything like my teachers then 'riotous behaviour' probably meant laughing out loud at a joke. (A rare event – teachers don't normally understand jokes.)
- In Oxford, England, one teacher's devotion to duty lead to a shocking end. If his pupils had written a diary then it might have looked like this . . .

> Dear Diary, today we had a terrible tragedy. Our school teacher Master Dicken, decided to thrash us all with the birch because Peter de Vere left a dead rat on his desk (It was meant to be a gift. Peter's funny like that.) Master Dicken began thrashing the first boy on the register Thomas Abbot and the birch twigs began to split. "Copy out Psalm 34 onto your wax tablets while I collect more birch twigs,"

Master Dicken told us. We went to the window and watched him march down the school garden to the river bank. All the branches hanging over the garden were dry and brittle. It has been a dry summer. The really springy hurting branches hung over the river. We watched, amazed, as he began to climb the tree and make his way out to the branches over the river. We counted as he cut ten, eleven, twelve whippy twigs. They do say thirteen is an unlucky number. As he cut number thirteen he lost his hold and tumbled into the water. His heavy gown soaked up the water and dragged him down. We raced out of the classroom and down the garden to get a better look. Master Dicken was waving at us. Each time his head came above the surface he waved. We waved back. At last his head went under one last time. We watched for another hour but saw no more of him. "I think he's in trouble," Peter de Vere said. "Shall we go for help?" he asked. "Give it another hour — just to be sure," I told him.

The teacher died. But death wasn't the only thing faced by teachers. There was worse! Damage to precious schoolbooks! One Middle Ages schoolteacher wrote a letter to a parent complaining of his son's greasy fingerprints and scribbled notes on his books not to mention . . .

> *In winter it is chilly, his nose runs, and he does not even bother to wipe it until it has dripped and dirtied the book.*

Groovy games you may like to play

At least children in the Middle Ages did have toys – like dolls with their own carriages. The carriages were pulled along by mice. (It's annoying opening a Christmas present today and finding it has dead batteries. Imagine opening one and finding it has dead mice!)

Children played games that are still played today – seesaws, swings, skipping, hide-and-seek, and follow-the-leader.

They also played some very rough games that you may not enjoy so much. Their Blind Man's Buff game was known as Hoodman Blind or Hot Cockles. A child would be 'It' and turn their hood around so it covered their face. They knelt on the ground with their hands behind their back while the others ran past and swiped the hands. If the hooded child guessed who had struck them then the striker became 'It' and so it went on.

Some games were played by adults as well as children. Games like . . .

Raffle 
You need:
- three dice
- a score sheet and pen

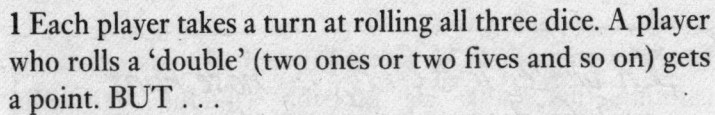

Rules:
1 Each player takes a turn at rolling all three dice. A player who rolls a 'double' (two ones or two fives and so on) gets a point. BUT . . .
2 If both players roll a double then the highest wins the point. (Double four beats double two, say.)
3 The first player to 10 points is the winner BUT . . .
4 Any player rolling three dice the same wins the whole game with that throw.

Kayles
You need:
- nine skittles (or plastic bottles of the sort used for powdered milk)
- a stick (or a 30 cm ruler)

Rules:
1 Place the skittles in a triangle with the point towards the thrower. The first row has one skittle, row two has two, row three has three and row four has four. (Even you can remember that!) The skittles should be fairly close so that if one falls it will knock over another one.

2 Agree a mark of 2 to 3 metres away from the skittles.
3 Each player throws the stick twice at the skittles.
4 The player who knocks over the most in two throws is the winner.

Note: Another arrangement is to place the skittles in a straight line facing you.

Extra note: In 1477 King Edward IV passed a law banning this game. He probably couldn't stand the thought of poor people enjoying themselves!

Gruesome games you wouldn't want to play

People enjoyed playing ghastly games. Some are still played and have hardly changed in the last 700 years . . .

Camp ball

The game was similar to football. You grabbed the ball and tried to get it into your opponent's goal a few dozen metres or a couple of miles apart. There were any number on each side and hardly any rules. The trouble was there were no football strips – players wore their normal clothes . . . including knives! In Newcastle-Upon-Tyne in 1280, Henry de Ellington ran into David le Keu. David was wearing a knife at his belt, the knife stabbed Henry in the gut and he died. Deadly David didn't get a red card but hacked Henry probably got a very red shirt.

Stool ball
A milkmaid sat on a three-legged stool. Measly men bowled a ball at her like skittles while she tried to dodge. If they hit her then they got a prize. But beware! The prizes were not gold medals. They were cakes . . . or kisses!

Ice jousting
Ice-skating was popular but the skates were made of animal bones strapped to the feet. The skaters didn't move their feet the way modern skaters do. They pushed

themselves along with poles (like skiers). This harmless sport became deadly when savage skaters charged at each other at speed and used the poles like knights' lances. Lots of broken poles but even more broken bones. Then there was the danger of thin ice.

Archaeologists dug up the skeleton of a woman from the bed of a river. Bone skates were still attached to the skeleton bones of her feet. No prizes for guessing what happened to her.

Snowballing
This popular game was probably played by cavemen. But the people of the Middle Ages had to think of a particularly nasty use for it. They used snowballs to pelt Earl Thomas of Lancaster . . . while he was being taken to his execution!

Middle Ages mind-benders

Pester your parents or torment your teachers with these questions. After all, those wrinklies are a few years nearer to the Middle Ages than you. They have a better chance of getting them right.

1 If you go to a wedding today then you may throw confetti over the bride for luck. In the Middle Ages the guests threw . . .
a) Grains of rice.
b) Tins of rice.
c) Sawdust.

2 Universities were wild places where one rule said . . .
a) It is forbidden to stick a knife in an examiner just because he asks you a hard question.
b) Students who get a question wrong must miss a day's food.
c) Cheeky students must write out 1000 times, 'I will obey.'

3 A miller in the Middle Ages dug clay from the middle of the road to mend his house. What happened next?

a) He was arrested and forced to fill in the hole with stones from the seashore ten miles away.

b) The hole filled with water after a storm and a travelling glove-maker fell in and drowned.

c) The local people took the clay back to the road and the miller's house fell down.

4 Superstitious people in the Middle Ages believed in monsters in far-off lands. One such monster was the Sciapod. He was a one-legged giant. But how did people say the Sciapod shaded himself from the sun?

a) With an umbrella made from the skins of human beings he had eaten.

b) He ripped up an oak tree, rested it on his shoulder and used the branches as a sun shade.

c) He lay on his back, stuck his leg in the air and sheltered under the shadow of his huge foot.

5 The Count of Armagnac argued with his wife over some property. How did he try to persuade her to sign it over?
a) Sent her a wagon-load of flowers, 20 new dresses and a barrel of perfume.
b) Broke a few of her bones and locked her away.
c) Placed a rope around his neck and threatened to jump off the castle roof.

6 In the Middle Ages many lords employed someone called a 'panter'. But what was a panter's job?
a) To look after the pantry in the castle kitchen.
b) To run through the forest (panting) and drive deer out for his lordship to shoot at.
c) To work in the tailor's shop making pants.

7 The peasants' revolt was led by a soldier called Wat Tyler. How did he get the name 'Wat'?
a) His parents christened him 'Wat'.
b) His initials W.A.T. stood for Wilfred Andrew Tyler and 'Wat' became his nickname.
c) Wat was short for Walter.

8 Boys at St Paul's school had to pee into large tubs. Why?
a) Because it was more hygienic.
b) Because the school could sell the urine to local leather workers for softening leather.
c) Because it was too far to the river-side toilets and they would miss lessons.

9 How did monks in the Middle Ages keep the bald patch (tonsure) in the middle of their heads?
a) They polished it with a piece of stone.
b) They singed the hair with a wax taper then dusted the ash off with a leather glove.
c) They pulled the hair out one strand at a time with tweezers.

10 Dick Whittington died in 1423 after twice being mayor of which town?
a) Storytown (because he never really existed).
b) London.
c) Calais.

Answers:
1c) Rice is an Asian crop not grown in England. If any did reach Britain in the Middle Ages then it would be far too precious to waste on a buxom bride! ('Buxom' meant 'obedient' because that's what a Middle Ages woman promised to be.)
2a) Students in Oxford became highwaymen to pay for their classes. The townspeople of Oxford responded by attacking the students – they killed and scalped quite a few! (Punishment **c)** was still being given to school pupils in the 1970s – but at least they had stopped scalping by then.)

3b) The miller took so much clay that the glove-maker rode into what looked like a puddle but was really deep enough to drown him . . . and his horse!

4c) And if any other Sciapods came along to disturb him then he'd tell them to hop it! (Only joking.)

5b) He was the sort of bully who gets his own way by putting somebody's eye in a sling.

6a) He worked with the ewerer (and if you were a ewerer you were a man in charge of washing the tablecloths and napkins) and with the spit boys (who spitted meat but didn't spit spittle) and with pot boys (who didn't have pot bellies).

7c) Wat Tyler was Walter Tyler. In fact the peasants mightn't have followed him if they'd known they were being led by a Wally.

8b) The school sold the urine and put the money they made towards the school fund. Many modern schools find ways to make money for the school fund. Has your school thought of this one?

9a) They used a type of stone called pumice stone – a sort of volcanic rock that is still sold today. People now use it in the bath to smooth off rough skin on the feet. (WARNING: If you find some in your bathroom, do not practise on your dad.)

10c) Dick Whittington was a real person. Everyone knows the story of Dick and his cat and the bells that said, 'Turn again Whittington and you shall be Lord Mayor of London three times.' BUT not a lot of people know that he was also Mayor of Calais – twice! Which just goes to show, eight out of ten cats (and Calais voters) prefer Whittington!

Rotten religion

People of the Middle Ages were pretty superstitious. They believed in almost anything supernatural, including ...

Ropey relics
Monasteries collected religious articles. They attracted visitors and were often said to perform miracles. Relics like a tooth of Saint Apollonia – the patron saint of toothache – could cure your tortured tootsie-peg. (Her teeth had been knocked out by the Romans before they burned her.) Hundreds of monasteries had a tooth from her mouth. Big mouth? No, simply another miracle, the monks explained. Henry VI of England collected a ton of them.

Why not start your own collection of saintly relics? Next time you cut your fingernails, save the clippings – that's what one group of measly monks did and said they belonged to St Edmund. Bones make very popular relics. (Your local butcher's shop may be able to help! Many travelling friars used pigs' bones to cheat people.)

Here are just ten 'relics' from churches and monasteries across Europe ...

- a piece of St Eustace's brain (wonder what it thought about being a relic?)

- wood from the manger in which Jesus was born and the cloth that the baby Jesus was wrapped in
- the coals on which St Lawrence was roasted
- Saint John's handkerchief (complete with Saintly snot)

- one of the stones used to stone St Stephen to death (bloodstained, naturally)
- a piece of the stone on which Jesus stood as he ascended to heaven
- a piece of bread chewed by Jesus
- the head of John the Baptist (Angers and Amiens Cathedrals both had one!)

- the crown of thorns placed on Jesus' head at his crucifixion
- a piece of wood from Jesus' cross (thousands of these).

All right, so I made up the handkerchief, but the others are all genuine relics! Or genuine fakes, but the believers took them seriously. Dead seriously. The monks of Conques pinched a saint's body from another monastery!

One saintly monk was terrified to hear that a monastery was planning to kill him and boil his body down so they could have his bones as relics – he changed his mind about visiting them.

Pay as you pray
In 1303 King Philip of France argued with the Italian Pope Boniface about who people should obey – kings or popes. Philip decided the matter by kidnapping 86-year-old Boniface from Rome. The Pope never recovered from the shock and died.

OH WELL, I SUPPOSE WE CAN STILL SELL HIM IN BITS AS RELICS

The next pope was a Frenchman called Clement. Wise Clement decided to stay in France – after all, the Italians might get their own back and kidnap him if he went to Rome. (There was also a little matter of Clement's girlfriend. He wanted to stay with her in France.)

Once the Pope and his headquarters moved to France they set about cashing in on their power. If you ever become Pope then here are a few measly Middle Ages ways of making money . . .

Religious rip-offs
1 If you commit a sin (like pinching a penny or pinching the bum of the girl in front of you) then the church can

'pardon' you . . . if you pay.

2 If you want to be important in the church (say, a cardinal because they get to wear a red cloak and you think red suits you) then you can have the job . . . if you pay.

3 If a church owns some very holy object (like the toe-nail of a saint or the feather from an angel's wing) then you can have it . . . if you pay.

4 If you give a gift to your local church (maybe money so the church will say prayers after you are dead), the Pope will take a share.

5 The Pope may raise a tax to pay for a Crusade (to fight against the non-Christians in the Holy Land) . . . you fork out, but he won't actually spend it on a Crusade.

6 If you want to be buried in two places at once (your heart in one place and your body in another, like Richard II) then you can have permission . . . if you pay.

7 If you want to marry a close relative (like your dead husband's brother) then you can have permission . . . if you pay.

8 If you are a nun and want to keep two maids (one to do your cleaning and one to do your praying, maybe?) then you can have permission . . . if you pay.

9 If you want to trade with those 'awful' non-Christian chaps from the East (and after all we do want their delicious spices, don't we?) then you can have permission . . . if you pay.

Potty plays

The local craftsmen formed themselves into groups called guilds. Around Easter the guilds came together to produce plays for the people – the masses. These plays were based on Bible stories: Miracle Plays and Mystery plays. That doesn't sound too measly – yet. The guilds performed the plays depending on their own mastery – so they called them mystery plays. Mastery-mystery, geddit?

At first these were performed at the altar of the church – but they became too popular and the churches were full of smelly people. So the plays were moved into the churchyards. But people began trampling on the graves to get a better view. In the end they were taken out of the churches and on to the streets.

The plays were always religious – but that didn't stop them being fun and horribly dangerous! In those days there was no one to give a 'rating' to the plays. Nowadays you know a film is a bit scary if it has a PG (Parental Guidance) rating. In the Middle Ages a lot of the plays were PG – Pretty Gruesome! Which of these horrors could be seen on stage in the Middle Ages?

1 John the Baptist having his head cut off.
2 Jesus being crucified.
3 Jesus rising from the dead and ascending into heaven (or the roof of the stage).
4 The tigers eating the hamsters on Noah's Ark.
5 The donkeys of the Three Wise Men leaving piles of dung droppings on the stage.
6 The Roman Emperor Nero slitting open his mother's stomach.
7 Adam and Eve appearing naked in the garden of Eden.
8 Judas hanging himself from a tree.

I DON'T KNOW...IT JUST DOESN'T SEEM AS ACTION PACKED AS IT USED TO BE

Answers:

1 True. At the last moment the actor was switched for a dummy. The fake neck was chopped, splitting a bag of ox blood that splashed into the audience.

2 True. The nails through the hands were faked but the suffering for the actor could still be quite nasty – he was tied up to the cross for as much as three hours ... while the actors playing Roman soldiers spat at him! A local priest played Jesus – and almost died on the cross!

3 True. A series of weights and pulleys were used to winch the actor up on a platform.

4 False. But Noah's Ark was very popular with floods from barrels of water and great drums of stones rumbled to make the sound of thunder. Noah was often shown as drunk and nearly naked.

5 True. The 'donkeys' were actors in a donkey skin. They pushed piles of manure out from under the tail!

6 True. It was a fake stomach, of course. When the sword split the skin, a bundle of pig's guts from the butcher spilled out on to the stage.

7 False. Adam could have played the part – Eve would have had a bit of a problem since all the actors were men!

8 True. An actor playing Judas 'hanged' himself at the end of the play ... and did it so well he almost died!

In 1326 the people of London turned against the Church because of the taxes it collected. They grabbed a bishop, cut his head off and left his naked body in the street – that was for real; no acting involved!

Batty beliefs
Medieval people believed that in faraway lands there were ...
- forests so high they touched the clouds
- tribes of people with horns who grow old in seven years
- men with the heads of dogs and six toes
- trees that grow wool

- cyclopeans with one eye and one foot who moved faster than the wind (when told to hop it)
- 100-metre snakes with jewels for eyes.

Eerie eggs.
Got a sickly sister or a plague-spotted pal? Want to know if they'll recover? The doctor would take a hen's egg and write the letters i, so, p, q, x, s, y, s, 9, o on the side. The egg was left in the open air overnight then cracked open in the morning. If there's blood in the egg then call the undertaker!

(Of course this is *nonsense*! But it meant the doctors could say, 'See! They are fated to die. Don't blame me – blame God . . . and here's my bill.')

Miserable monks
Life was unpleasant for peasants. As the Middle Ages went on, some were able to move from the land to the towns which were starting to grow. After the Black Death the Feudal System began to fall apart. Peasants became free to sell their labour or to move.

In towns they could become craftsmen or traders. They weren't tied to the land by the old Feudal System and some grew rich as merchants. But for others the only way out of the measly miserable life on the land was to join the church. Boys and girls as young as seven could be taken on as monks or nuns.

At first the young trainee monks were called novices – a bit like learner drivers in cars today, they weren't allowed to go out on their own. But it was a very hard life . . . even harder than school today! Some of the mini-monks must have had a miserable time . . .

> Dear Mum,
> Hope you can get someone in the village to read this to you. The fact is, I want to come home. It's horrible here and I miss your rabbit pies.
> It all starts at 2 in the morning. First prayers. That awful bell wakes us up,

and I have to put on my sandals. I don't have to dress because we sleep in our robes — and they're rotten and itchy. Last night I stumbled into the back of old Brother Benedict. He whipped me with a cane. Have you ever tried praying for two hours with a burning backside?

I got back to bed at 4 and slept two hours — on my face, of course — then that bell's ringing again to call us off to Prime service at 6. Brother Benedict breaks the ice on the water trough and makes me wash. He says it will stop me falling asleep. It just freezes my cheeks. Did you know the Benedictine monks pray at least eight times a day? I asked old Benedict if God wouldn't want us to stop so he could get some sleep. He whipped me — Benedict, that is, not God.

We get breakfast at 7. It's usually porridge. Thin, cold, gritty porridge. Except this morning brother Edward stood on my toe and I cried out. We aren't allowed to make a noise at meals. I was whipped and told I'd eat bread and water for three days. I'd rather have your rabbit pies.

At 8 it's the meeting in the Chapter House — but the novices don't get a word in while the old goats groan on about money and work. It ends with prayers for the dead. But Mum... I don't know anybody that's dead. I sometimes wish I was dead though. Heaven has to be warmer than this place.

After Terce service at 9 we work. It was writing practice in the scriptorium for me. Brother Eamon makes us write on vellum — that's skins taken from the bellies of calves. I wonder why God wants us to do that? This letter's written on the belly of a calf, but I didn't kill it. I can't hold the goose-feather pen in my cold hands. I make smadges and Brother Eamon beats me.

It's High Mass at 11 then off to the fields to work. I had to dig cow muck into the soil. The smell would have made me sick, if I'd had any food in my stomach.

I'm almost glad to get indoors for the None service at 3 then it's lessons till Vespers at 6. I had to sit next to Anthony and I argued with him. He gets beaten as hard as me so I didn't feel too bad. Just hungry.

Compline at 7 and I have bread and water while the other monks eat peas with herbs. That tastes worse than bread and water. Every day, peas and herbs, peas and herbs. Sometimes I imagine I have herbs and peas for a change.

At 8 I have a little time to write this before I go to bed and it starts all over again at 2 tomorrow morning. Just let me come home, Mum, and I promise I'll be the best son you've ever had. I'll walk all the way, I'll pay back the gift that you gave to the monks when they took me in. Just let me come home Mum. I do miss your rabbit pies. Please, Mum.

Your loving son,

Arthur

Mischievous monks

The monks can't all have been saints because rules were written down to say what monks must NOT do. So somebody must have done these terrible things or they wouldn't have had to have the rules! Some of the rules look rather similar to school rules!

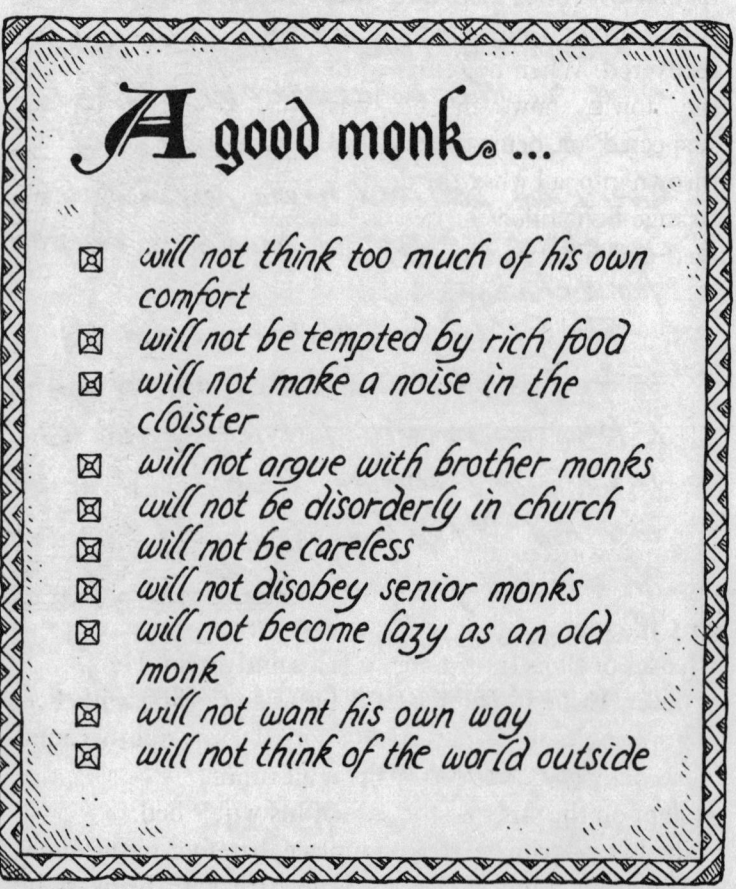

A good monk ...

- ☒ will not think too much of his own comfort
- ☒ will not be tempted by rich food
- ☒ will not make a noise in the cloister
- ☒ will not argue with brother monks
- ☒ will not be disorderly in church
- ☒ will not be careless
- ☒ will not disobey senior monks
- ☒ will not become lazy as an old monk
- ☒ will not want his own way
- ☒ will not think of the world outside

Rules for nuns were very similar. How would *you* have survived?

St Roch

People who caught the plague used to call upon the spirit of St Roch for help. Roch caught the plague when he was a young man and went to a wood to die. A dog brought him food and he recovered. When he returned to the town, however, he was suspected of being a spy and thrown into jail where he died. A strange light filled the cell as he died and his captors believed it was a miracle. They decided that if you called for his help then you'd be cured of the plague. On the other hand you may *not* be cured of the plague! This was not St Roch's fault. This was because God decided you had been too wicked.

St Charles

Charles of Blois (in France) was a saintly man. He . . .

- never washed his clothes so he was crawling with lice, put pebbles in his shoes and knotted cords tightly round his body so he suffered pain at all times.
- slept on the straw at the side of his wife's bed.
- made a pilgrimage to a holy place, barefoot in the snow. When his admirers covered the path with blankets he took another road and walked till his feet were frozen and bleeding.

Charles of Blois was a vicious and cruel man. He . . .
- used large catapults to hurl the heads of dead prisoners into an enemy city.
- massacred 2,000 men, women and children when he captured a town called Quimper.

Cruelty alongside saintliness. That pretty well sums up the measly Middle Ages.

Epilogue

Richard III was killed at the Battle of Bosworth Field in 1485. His body was stripped and paraded in public for two days. That was the sort of gruesome spectacle the people of the Middle Ages would have enjoyed.

But things were changing. In England Henry Tudor began a new era – that of the terrible Tudors. The English had been invaded by the Normans, and seen Matilda and Stephen fight a civil war for the crown. The barons had rebelled against King John then gone to war with Henry in another war. Then the country went into a Hundred Years War with France at the same time as it was ravaged by the terrible Black Death. No sooner had the Hundred Years War finished than the vicious Wars of the Roses tore the country apart.

At last Henry Tudor brought a new and wonderful gift to the English people. Peace. And in those peaceful few years the people were able to enjoy life a little more. They became 'civilized'. Life was never quite the same crude, rough, dangerous (and short) thing it had been.

That's why some historians draw the line at the Battle of Bosworth Field and say, 'That was the end of the Middle Ages.' Of course nothing's ever that simple or neat. But things were happening in the rest of the world that meant change was on the way. Just a few years later, in 1492, a bloke called Columbus discovered America. Then Henry Tudor's son, Henry VIII, cut England's links with the Catholic Church and the Pope in Rome.

By the time slimy Stuart king James I united England with her old enemy, Scotland, in 1603, those old days of the measly Middle Ages seemed a world away.

But a clever Frenchman called Voltaire said, 'History never repeats itself . . . humans always do.' The cruelty and stupidity and superstition of the Middle Ages should be a distant nightmare. Yet in the 20th century people can still find ways of making life miserable for others. Bullies with muscles, bullies with money or bullies with power. Just read today's newspapers.

Until they stop we are not really out of the Middle Ages. We're still living in them.

MEASLY MIDDLE AGES

GRISLY QUIZ

Now find out if you're a
measly Middle Ages expert!

MIDDLE AGES MIND-BENDERS

A muddled monk wrote these facts about the Middle Ages. But he jumbled the words and he added one word to each sentence that doesn't belong there! Can you sort the words into the right order? (Clue: the odd word out is always in the same position in the sentence)

> KNOW HOW YOU HARD WHEN IT'S NOT REALLY TROUT

1. Brides threw over the guests sawdust wedding cake.
2. Teachers were allowed to stab their students not Mondays.
3. A rider road and drowned his horse in a hole in the head.
4. An umbrella used his foot as a giant single snail.
5. The Count of Armagnac broke his bones in a wife's row boat.
6. A pantry looked panter after the castle crumbled.
7. Walter Tyler's proper rebel name was Wat luck.
8. Barrel boys' at St Paul's school collected a pee in the teachers hats.
9. Heads polished their stone with a monks habit.
10. Calais Dick Whittington was twice mayor of London.

CLUELESS CURES

The people of the 1300s didn't know how to cure the plague but made some weird guesses. Which of the following did they actually try?

1. Sniff scented flowers.
2. Kill all the town's cats and dogs.
3. Wear a magpie's beak around your neck.
4. Build huge bonfires in the street to burn the bad air.
5. Drill a hole in your head to let out evil spirits.
6. Don't drink from any well because it could be poisoned.
7. Sleep on your side because sleeping on your back lets foul air run into your nose.
8. Drink cream mixed with the blood from a black cat's tail.
9. Eat onions, leeks and garlic.
10. Eat ten-year-old treacle mixed with marigold flowers and powdered egg.
11. Stop having baths or shaves or a change of clothes.
12. Run away to the countryside where the air is fresh.
13. Throw sweet-smelling herbs on a fire to clean the air.
14. Sit in a sewer so the bad air of the plague is driven off by the worse air of the drains.

PERHAPS THE PLAGUE'S NOT SO BAD AFTER ALL

15. Swallow powders of crushed emeralds.
16. Eat arsenic powder.
17. Try letting blood out of your body (when your horoscope is right).
18. Shave a live chicken's bottom and strap it to the plague sore.
19. March from town to town flogging yourself with a whip to drive out devils.

Weird Words

Books began to be printed in English and people could read the horrible sufferings of the peasants – though the peasants themselves probably wouldn't have been able to read. William Langland wrote a poem about a peasant called 'Piers Ploughman' and his miserable life. Can you work out just how miserable from this part of the poem? Some of the words have been scrambled by a careless printer – well, the first book printed in English was produced in 1475, so he hadn't had a lot of practice.

The Peasant
His coat of a cloth that is NITH (1) as the East wind,
His DOHO (2) full of holes with his HARI (3) sticking through,
His clumsy HOSSE (4), knobbled and nailed over thickly,
Yet his SOTE (5) poked clean through as he trod on the ground.
Two miserable mittens made out of old GRAS (6),
The fingers worn out and the FHLIT (7) caked on them,
He waded in mud almost up to his KLANSE (8),
In front are four NOXE (9), so weary and feeble
Their BRIS (10) could be counted, so wretched they were.

Quick Questions

1. In 1301 King Edward I's son, Edward, was proclaimed a prince. But he wasn't proclaimed Prince of England. Instead he was named prince of where? (Clue: not the Prince of Dolphins)

2. Edward I brought law and order to England. How did they say he dealt with a leading outlaw who was robbing travellers? (Clue: king of the road)

3. In 1314 the Scots were still fighting the new English king, Edward II. Scot James Douglas captured Roxburgh castle with a trick. What? (Clue: hide in places!)

4. In 1337 Edward III claimed to be King of France. The French disagreed and the Hundred Years War started. How long did it last? (Clue: not a hundred years!)

5. In 1376 Edward III died and ten-year-old Richard II was crowned the following year. He walked into Westminster but was carried out. Why? (Clue: zzzzz)

6. One of the curious rumours that was going around was that Richard II was born without what? (Clue: you can have sausages like this, but not humans)

7. In 1381 Richard's government charged an unpopular 'Poll Tax' of four pence for every person. A rebellion was led by a man called Tyler. What was his first name? (Clue: Yes, it is!)

8. The end of the century brought the end for Richard II.

In September 1399 he was forced to give up his throne to Henry IV. If he burst into tears then something he had invented would come in useful. What? (Clue: who nose if he really did invent it?)

9. The 1400s were just six days old when Richard II died. He had been a prisoner of the new king, Henry IV. How did Richard die? (Clue: he has no stomach for a fight)

10. Henry V took the throne in 1413 and married Catherine. Two hundred and thirty years later the writer Samuel Pepys kissed her. How? (Clue: everyone likes a kiss from their mummy)

11. Henry VI sat at the head of his parliament. But he sat where no English king has sat before or since. Where? (Clue: another kiss from mummy)

Answers

Middle Ages Mind-benders
1. Wedding guests threw sawdust over the brides. (If you go to a wedding today then you might throw confetti over the bride for luck. In the Middle Ages the guests threw sawdust.)
2. Students were not allowed to stab their teachers. (It was forbidden to knife an examiner just because he asked you a hard question!)
3. A rider and his horse drowned in a hole in the road. (A miller dug clay from the middle of the road to mend his house. The hole filled with water after a storm and a travelling glove-maker fell in and drowned – along with his horse.)

4. A giant used his single foot as an umbrella. (Superstitious people believed in monsters, such as the one-legged 'Sciapod'. He lay on his back stuck his leg in the air and sheltered under the shadow of his huge foot.)

5. The Count of Armagnac broke his wife's bones in a row. (He was trying to persuade her to sign over some land. After beating her he threw her in a dungeon. This was gentle persuasion.)

6. A panter looked after the castle pantry. (He could have been named after the place where he worked – or he could have been a panter because he had to run up and down all those castle stairs!)

7. Rebel Wat Tyler's proper name was Walter. (He could have been called a Wally.)

8. Teachers at St Paul's school collected the boys' pee in a barrel. (It was sold to leather workers to soften the leather. So if your shoes are hard and uncomfortable, you know what to do? Limp.)

9. Monks polished their heads with a stone. (It was a stone called a 'pumice'. The slaphead monks would have used sandpaper if it had been invented.)

10. Dick Whittington was twice mayor of Calais. (Dick Whittington was a real person. Everyone knows the story of Dick and his cat and the bells that said, 'Turn again Whittington and you shall be Lord Mayor of London three times.' BUT not a lot of people know that he was also mayor of Calais – twice!

Clueless Cures
1–19. ALL are true except 3 (a cure for toothache), 5 (a cure for a headache) and 8 (a cure for a cough).

Weird Words
1) Thin 2) Hood 3) Hair 4) Shoes 5) Toes 6) Rags
7) Filth 8) Ankles 9) Oxen 10) Ribs

Quick Questions
1. Prince of Wales. It's a title that has been given to an English monarch's oldest son ever since.
2. Ed rode out and took on the outlaw in a fight. He beat him and made the road safe. (This is probably not a true story, though)
3. His soldiers disguised themselves as cattle! Under the cover of the skins they got close enough to surprise the guards.
4. 116 years.
5. Richard collapsed under the strain of the excitement – and the heavy robes and crown.
6. A skin! He was supposed to have been wrapped in a goat skin to save his life! Weird.
7. Wat.
8. The Handkerchief.
9. He starved himself to death, some said. Others said he'd been starved on the orders of the king.
10. Catherine's corpse was turned into a mummy and put on show next to the coffin of Henry V. People could look at her for a couple of pennies and she stayed there for almost 300 years. Samuel Pepys kissed the mummy – weird!
11. Henry sat on him mum's knee. He was just eight months old when he took the throne. Some days he had such screaming fits that his visits to parliament had to be cancelled.

INTERESTING INDEX

Where will you find 'brewed beetles', 'bottom-shaved chickens', 'ten-year-old treacle' and 'toads' in an index? In a Horrible Histories book, of course!

D'Abrissel, Robert (priest) 83
ale 66-9
Alfred the Great (king of Wessex) 7
amputations 57
Angevins 52-61, 73
Anglo-Saxons 93
Apollonia (saint) 112
archaeologists 106
archers 49, 74-7, 79, 95
Arthur of Brittany (French prince) 60
Arthur (mythical king) 42

Bannockburn, Battle of 75-6, 79
barons 8, 53, 61, 127
beavers 62
Beckett, Thomas à (archbishop of Canterbury) 55
beetles, brewed 39
beggars 57, 95
Benedictine monks 121
Black Death (bubonic plague) 9, 12, 20, 30-6, 120, 127
De Born, Bertrand (Middle Ages pop singer) 81
Bosworth Field, battle of 9, 77-8, 127

branks (head cages) 59
brains, dashed out 59
bunions 85
Burgundy 90
bustards 62
butchers 67, 71, 112, 118

cabbage soup 63-4
Cale, Will (peasant) 22-4, 27
cannibalism 14
Canute/Knut (king of England) 7
Charles of Blois (monk) 125-6
Charles of Navarre (king of Navarre) 23-4
Chickens, bottom-shaved 33
Church 62, 66, 83-4, 114-16, 118, 120, 124, 127
Clarence, Duke of 68
De Clisson, Jeanne (French wife) 87-8
De Clisson, Olivier (French husband) 87
coals, roasting on 112
Columbus, Christopher (Italian explorer) 10, 127
Crécy, battle of 76-7, 79-80, 91
crimes 52-6
crossbows 77, 79, 90

crowns
  of red-hot iron 58
  of thorns 113
crusades 8, 50, 60, 115
cures 32-3, 37-9

Damien (doctor) 40-1
Dark Ages 7, 11-12
David (king of Scotland) 54
Denville, Gosseline (outlaw) 54, 56
doctors 32-3, 36-41, 119-20
Domesday Book 8, 27
duels 58

Edmund (saint) 112
Edward II (king of England) 9, 75-6
Edward III (king of England) 9, 42, 76, 90-1
Edward IV (king of England) 68, 104
Edward (king of England) 12
Eleanor (English queen) 60
Elizabeth of York (English queen) 73
English language 97-8
Eustace (saint) 112
ewerers (tablecloth washers) 111

fashions 84-7
feudal system 19-29, 120
flagellants (self-floggers) 35-6
De Folville brothers (criminals) 54-5
forgery 57
Fulk (lord of Anjou) 85

games
  groovy 102-4
  gruesome 104-6
Geoffrey (king of Brittany) 11
Geoffrey (prince) 60
Godiva (countess/tax protester) 28-9
guilds 116

guts 67, 71, 105, 118

Hackford, John de (liar) 58
hangovers, cure for 39
Harold (Saxon king) 7, 12, 74, 79
Hastings, battle of 11, 74, 79
hats, steeple 85-6
hawking (hunting with hawks, falcons etc) 58, 59, 91
heads 8, 39, 113, 116
  in cages 58
  in catapults 126
  cut off 81, 116, 118
  on poles 53
hedgehogs 62, 76
Henry I (king of England) 17-18, 52
Henry II (king of England) 52-3, 55, 57, 59-60
Henry III (king of England) 8, 60, 127
Henry IV (king of England) 73
Henry VI (king of England) 73, 80, 112
Henry VII (king of England) 9-10, 73, 77-8, 80, 127
Henry VIII (king of England) 69, 127
highwaymen, students as 110
Hockele, William (toilet-builder) 71
Hood, Robin (mythical outlaw) 53-4
Hundred Years War 9, 76, 127

Ice Age, Little 8

Jacquerie (French peasants) 22-4
James I (king of Scotland) 58
James IV (king of Scotland) 40
James VI/I (king of Scotland/England) 127
Jeanne la Pucelle see Joan of Arc
jesters 48-50
Joan of Arc (French heroine) 9, 90
John the Baptist (saint) 113, 116
John of Gaddesden (beetle brewer) 39

138

John (king) 8, 59-60, 127

kings 19-20, 42, 52-4, 114
knights 13, 19, 22-3, 25, 42-9
   attacking 74, 77
   bold 28-9, 40, 50, 55
   charging 75-6
   giving up 82
   lances 106
   trampled by 79-80
   tunics 85

Lancaster family (red rose warriors) 9, 73-82
Latin (Roman language) 53, 61, 98
Lawrence (saint) 112
lepers 32
limb-breaking 95
longbows 77, 79

magic, black 54
Magna Carta (human rights charter) 8, 61
manners, mucky 69-70
De Marle, Thomas (French knight) 29
marriage 66, 83, 91-2, 115
Matilda (queen of England) 127
Matilda (William I's wife) 15, 17
minstrels (entertainers) 50
monasteries 54, 91, 112-14
monks 12, 55-6, 84-6, 91
   bald patches 110-11
   body snatching 113
   mischievous 124
   miserable 120-3
   relics 112, 114
De Montfort, John (French warrior) 89
De Montfort, Madame (French warrior) 89
De Montfort, Simon (rebel baron) 8

Nero (Roman emperor) 116

Noah (flood survivor) 9, 116, 118
Normans 7, 11-19, 27, 42, 60, 79, 122, 127
   Conquest 74
novices (trainee monks) 120, 122

Odo (William the Conqueror's brother) 14-15

panters (pantry workers) 109
peasants 5, 42, 53-4, 69
   becoming monks 120
   revolting 21-9, 109, 111
   value of 20, 59
Pedro I, the Cruel (king of Castile, Spain) 91
pee 37-8, 91, 109
Peter of Clarendon (thief) 57
Philip II (king of France) 60
Philip IV, the Fair (king of France) 87-8, 114
Philip VI (king of France) 49, 76-7, 79-80
Phoebus, Gaston (French knight) 23
pikes (poles to fight with) 75-6, 79
pillories ('stretch-necks') 58, 67-8
plays 116-19
poison 32-3, 83
Poll Tax rebellion 25-6

relics, ropey 112-14
rent collectors 54
Richard (earl of Warwick) 69
Richard I (king of England) 60
Richard II (king of England) 25-6, 73, 115
Richard III (king of England) 9, 73, 77-8, 80, 127
Richard (William the Conqueror's son) 18
Robert the Bruce (king of Scotland) 75, 79
Robert (count of Artois) 21
Robert (William the Conqueror's son) 15, 17-18
Roch (saint) 125
Roger of Wendover (writer) 28
Romans, rotten 7, 11, 112, 118
rose pudding 64-5

Roses, Wars of 9, 73, 77, 80, 127
Rummyng, Eleanor (brewer) 67-8
Runcorn, Ann (scold) 59

sacrifices 54
St Anthony's Fire (disease) 21
Saxons 11
school 22, 97
  dinners 33
Sciapod (giant) 108, 111
sewers, sitting in 32
sheep's feet, tasty 67
shoes
  platform 86
  pointy 85
skulls, holes in 32, 40
slaves 19, 26
Sluys, battle of 49
snot 102
Stanley, Lord (army commander) 78, 80
Stephen (king of England) 52, 127
Stephen (saint) 113
stocks 57
Stuarts 127
Suffolk, Duke of 80-1
swearing 59, 96

taxes 8, 19, 25-8, 61, 66, 115, 118
teachers 5-6, 11, 39, 52-3
  angry 38
  drowning 101
  letters from 102
  tormented 107
teeth
  aching 32
  patron saint of 112
  rotten 21, 64
Thomas of Lancaster (earl) 106
tights 84

toads 37, 39
toilets 71-2
tonsures (monks' bald patches) 110
treacle, ten-year old 32
troubadours (singers) 81
Tudor, Henry see Henry VII
Tudors 9-10, 57, 69, 73, 77-8, 80, 127
tunics 84
Tyler, Wat (peasant) 25-7, 109, 111

urine 32, 72, 109, 111

vellum (calf-skin paper) 122
Vikings 7, 11
villeins (peasant slaves) 19
Voltaire (French writer) 128

Walworth, William (mayor of London) 27
wars 74, 76-7, 81-2, 127-8
Whittington, Dick (mayor) 110-11
William I, the Conqueror (king of England) 7-8, 11-18, 27, 52, 74
William II, Rufus (king of England) 16-18
witches 9, 83, 90
Wulfstan (saint) 58
Wytte, Thomas (toilet-builder) 71

York family (White Rose warriors) 9, 73, 77

Terry Deary was born at a very early age, so long ago he can't remember. But his mother, who was there at the time, says he was born in Sunderland, north-east England, in 1946 – so it's not true that he writes all *Horrible Histories* from memory. At school he was a horrible child only interested in playing football and giving teachers a hard time. His history lessons were so boring and so badly taught, that he learned to loathe the subject. *Horrible Histories* is his revenge.

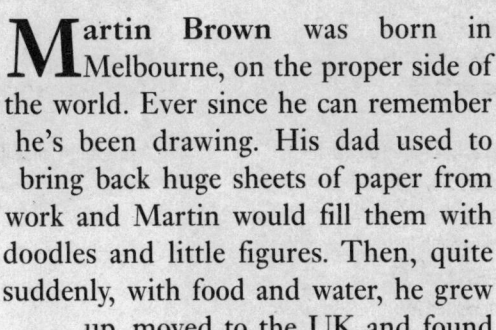

Martin Brown was born in Melbourne, on the proper side of the world. Ever since he can remember he's been drawing. His dad used to bring back huge sheets of paper from work and Martin would fill them with doodles and little figures. Then, quite suddenly, with food and water, he grew up, moved to the UK and found work doing what he's always wanted to do: drawing doodles and little figures.

Make sure you've got the whole horrible lot!

HORRIBLE HISTORIES
AWESOME EGYPTIANS
Terry Deary & Peter Hepplewhite
Illustrated by Martin Brown
ISBN: 978 0439 94403 8 £4.99

HORRIBLE HISTORIES
VICIOUS VIKINGS
Terry Deary Illustrated by Martin Brown
ISBN: 978 0439 94406 9 £4.99

HORRIBLE HISTORIES
ROTTEN ROMANS
Terry Deary Illustrated by Martin Brown
ISBN: 978 0439 94400 7 £4.99

HORRIBLE HISTORIES: WOEFUL SECOND WORLD WAR
Terry Deary, Illustrated by Martin Brown
ISBN: 978 0439 94399 4 £4.99

HORRIBLE HISTORIES: VILE VICTORIANS
Terry Deary, Illustrated by Martin Brown
ISBN: 978 0439 94404 5 £4.99

HORRIBLE HISTORIES: TERRIBLE TUDORS
Terry Deary & Neil Tonge, Illustrated by Martin Brown
ISBN: 978 0439 94406 9 £4.99

HORRIBLE HISTORIES: GROOVY GREEKS
Terry Deary, Illustrated by Martin Brown
ISBN: 978 0439 94402 1 £4.99

HORRIBLE HISTORIES HANDBOOKS

Pirates
IN BLOOD-CURDLING COLOUR!
Terry Deary Illustrated by Martin Brown
ISBN: 978 0439 95578 2 £5.99

HORRIBLE HISTORIES HANDBOOKS

Warriors
Terry Deary
ISBN: 978 0439 94330 7 £5.99

HORRIBLE HISTORIES HANDBOOKS

Knights
Terry Deary Illustrated by Martin Brown
ISBN: 978 0439 95577 5 £5.99

Don't miss these horribly handy handbooks for all the gore and more!